This book is dedicated to "Our Allie."

With Love from Her Devoted Family

Joe, Jeannie, Bryan, Chris, & Joe Jr. Rivera

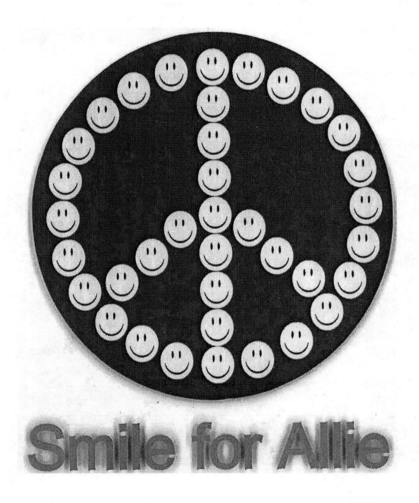

Library of Congress Control Number   2012906139

ISBN: 978-0-692-01739-5

Table of Contents

Poetry _____ 163

Foreword

Many young people are overlooked these days. Their ideas and dreams are often discounted by society merely because of their age and limited life experiences. One such young person is our daughter and sister, Allison Rivera. Allie's life was tragically cut short, but in her 18 years she lived life to its fullest and shared experiences that many people will never come to enjoy.

Allie had countless interests including journalism, debating, environmental activism, and animal rights. Allie was applying to colleges and planned to pursue a career in veterinary medicine. Just recently she had been awarded an academic scholarship to study Animal Science at the University of Illinois. However it was her passion for reading and writing that captured her real essence.

One of Allie's teachers and mentors described her as a joy-bringer. As her family, we hope you get a glimpse of the happiness she brought to every life she touched. The book culminates her views, feelings, and desires as described in her own words. The publication of these writings is a labor of love undertaken by the family and friends of Allie to ensure her memory is alive and will never be forgotten. [1]

As a person, Allie is gone....... but as an author her journey has just begun.

We pray that her writings will spread joy and comfort for all who she continues to touch.

---

[1] The Rivera Family and Friends would like to express our heartfelt thanks and appreciation to our editors, Tawnie Cisneros and Bill Lindich. Without your effort, this would not have been possible.

Editor's Note

Allison Rivera kept more than two dozen journals in just 18 years. Hundreds of pages of stories, essays and poetry, all in her girlish handwriting. Scribbles and doodles exorcising the wrong words and conjuring up the right. Her prolific writings tell us she took her work as a writer seriously.

She referred to herself as "Allison Wonderland," and her stories reflect the magic, fantasy and dreams that are the hallmarks of a rich imagination. As I read her journals, I could see her hand moving across the page, too fast for the pencil she favored, the words running together as her stories picked up speed. Like so many great authors, she was more concerned with telling a story than with the syntax of paragraphs, perfect spelling, or punctuation. In this edition, we've edited lightly, leaving her work just as she did – unapologetically imperfect, innocent and full of potential.

Allison wrote without self-consciousness, that fertile ground that so many authors (me included) find elusive and fleeting. Simply, she wrote as though she didn't have time to waste.

And sadly, though none of us knew it, she didn't. Allison died on October 22, 2011, just months after her 18th birthday. An undiagnosed cardio-thoracic problem swept her away down the rabbit hole. In one of her stories, this may have been a cover for a naughty sea nymph bearing her away to a new life as royalty in the fathoms below; or maybe a young woman reborn into the strong body of a lion, free to roam in a new dimension, though she'd left our own.

In our world, it simply meant we lost her. And it hurts. But to read Allison's stories is to hear her voice again, to feel the energy and promise that only a teenage girl can channel. So we've collected her work here to share Allison's Wonderland with everyone who craves a little magic.

Short Stories

A Trip to New York[2]

The feeling of adventure stays with a young person for a very long time. At age twelve my dad announced that we would be taking a vacation to New York. Never being to a big city, besides Chicago, I was ecstatic. When thinking back, I realize what a huge influence that trip had on me.

Plane rides have always been an exciting experience for me. Out the window, I gasped at the bright lights of New York City. Giddy with anticipation, I completely forgot my weariness and took in the lights and interesting things around me. Of course the airport was just about the same as any other. However, when I looked at the bright lights of Time Square, I knew that I was somewhere special.

The noise, the people, the city engulfed us as we left our hotel that night. "So how do you like the city?" my dad asked as we walked along the teeming sidewalks in Time Square.

"I love it," I beamed up at him. How could one place hold so much? The whole mass of people around me was amazing, and it made me somewhat wary on the outside. People on the streets passed me without a glance as I shrunk close to my father's side, trying to stay out of the constant traffic of people. On the inside, though, I was whirling.

I could say that my favorite part of that trip was the shopping, or the museum, or the Broadway play, though I think it had to be the feeling of being somewhere new and exciting, having my own adventure. Feeling amazingly special, when really I doubt anyone even noticed me.

It is understandable why people hate the city: too much noise, rude people, the smell of car fumes. I think a different way: a symphony of sound,

---

[2] "A Trip to New York" was a short essay written for Allison's Writing 2A class on September 8, 2009.

interesting people, and the delicious smell of food being sold on the streets. That visit taught me that there is more to life than just Illinois, and I intend to discover the wonder of it all.

Since then I have been to Mexico, Hawaii, Washington, Georgia, Tennessee, New Jersey, and Florida. When I am older, I intend to travel across the world. But above all, no matter where I may go, New York will always be my favorite because it was the first big place I visited, and it made a huge impact on me.

NY Girl @ Heart

Excerpt from Allie's Journals

Golopokis

Things about a Golopokis[3]

What is it:
mammal
long snout for smelling things miles away
spikes for protection
spike on its tail for protection
spot on its belly
very, very long

What it does: Spot is its mood
red = mad,
blue = sad,
pink = nappy,
black = sleepy,
purple = playful,
green = hungry

Where it is:
Located on the top of Mt. Everest
Lives in caves

What it eats:
Snow (mostly)
Grass
Any human food

Endangered
No threat
Being hunted
Only 1 family left

---

[3] Allie's original journal entry includes direction for the placement of this page: "This goes at the beginning." We've followed her plan in this publication.

Golopokis = Saphire

Bunny = Bunny

Deer = Hunny

It was still dawn when Saphire came out of her cave. Her and her family were the last of the Golopokises. If any hunters saw them they would kill them. Golopokises were thought to be very dangerous, but in reality they did no harm to anyone.

Saphire took a big bite of snow for breakfast. She always loved fresh snow. Her little sister Ruby was just waking up. Her father (Emerald) and mother (Diamond) were still sleeping. As Saphire gazed at the sunrise she thought about the world below. The world she knew nothing about. She longed seeing how humans lived.

Her sister was 2 months old and she was 9. Tomorrow was her 10th birthday. Her father always got her something from the human world.

For her 1st birthday he got her a ball.

2nd he got her a puppet.

3rd he got her a bow.

4th he got her a bracelet.

5th he got her a brush.

6th he got her a mirror.

7th he got her a book.

8th he got her a necklace

9th he got her a blanket.

And for her 10th birthday (she saw it in the cave) he got her a scarf. She was sooooo excited. She was going to have a birthday party with all her animal friends.

Bunny (she knew since she was born) was her best best friend. She went to school with her. One day at school she told Bunny that she wanted to go down to the human world.

"Are you crazy," said Bunny, "If they catch you they will kill you."

"Please, please, please, come with me," begged Saphire.

"Of course I'll come with you," said Bunny. "I mean I'm your best friend."

"Thank you soooo much," said Saphire. "I couldn't do this alone."

So at midnight they met under the oak tree by her cave. "I left a note for my parents," said Saphire.

"Me too," said Bunny. And with that they were gone.

All night they climbed down from Mt. Everest. They camped at the bottom and waited for morning.

At sunrise they woke up and ate grass. Saphire only ate snow so grass was all new to her. "Yuck," said Saphire making a horrible face.

"Come on," said Bunny, "it isn't all that bad. You'll get used to it."

"I'm gonna have to," said Saphire taking another bite.

After breakfast they headed for the nearest town being very careful not to be seen. They saw these big metal cars zooming past. And everyone was walking down the street.

They went into a clothes store and got a big overcoat, huge sunglasses and a fake mustache. Bunny would stand on Saphire's head and Saphire would stand on her back legs. They would put on those things and walk around town.

Nearby they went to a park and found some credit cards (in someone's purse) and checked in to the nearest hotel.

"Are you sure you're from around here," said the clerk.

"Of course," said Bunny. Once upstairs they took off their things.

"Wow," said Saphire, looking around, "this place is amazing!"

"Look at this thing," said Bunny. As they stared at the TV, there was a knock at the door. "Hold on," yelled Bunny, as they quickly put on their things.

"I just wanted to see how things were up here," said the clerk.

"Fine," said Bunny, "just fine."

When the clerk left Bunny and Saphire saw a pamphlet on the table marked Arizona.

"My cousin lives there," said Bunny.

"Well," said Saphire, "let's go there."

Bunny and Saphire (in their costume) took a taxi to the airport. On the plane Bunny pulled out what appeared to be a flower. "Happy Birthday," she said.

"This is sooooo nice," said Saphire. She had completely forgotten it was her birthday today. And with this rose she felt happy.

"Get down Saphire I just heard these two men talking."

"Ok," the first man said, "we'll catch them and skin them, then sell their skins."

"I love hunting lizards," said the second man.

"Oh no," thought Saphire, "they're going to kill the last of the Arizona lizards."

                              ***

When they landed it was the next day. Saphire told Bunny what she had heard on the plane. "That is horrible," said Bunny.

"We need to stop them," said Saphire.

So when the two men got into their car Saphire and Bunny got into a cab and followed them. They stopped at an abandoned warehouse in the middle of nowhere. As they peeked into a window they saw something horrible. Hundreds upon hundreds of Arizona lizards in cages ready to be skinned.

"Let's go in there and set them free," said Saphire. "Yeah," said Bunny.

So at midnight they went back and snuck into the warehouse. As Saphire comforted the lizards, Bunny found the keys and started unlocking the cages.

"Go free, go free!" they yelled. Suddenly they heard a yell.

"Oh no," said the men who caged these lizards up. "Our lizards!" they yelled, "everything is ruined."

"Wait," said the first man grabbing Saphire. "Do you know what this is?"

"Yes," said the second man, "It's the legendary Golopokis. This can be our big break!"

So they caged up Saphire while Bunny hid behind some boxes. The next morning Bunny got the keys and let Saphire out. But just as they got out the two men came back. So Saphire and Bunny made a run for it. So the chase was on. They ran through parks, apartments, and other public places. Saphire was so fast she out ran them and managed to stay hidden. They went deep into the woods. But this wasn't any ordinary woods. It was an enchanted forest. They realized they had run out of the city and into a cave. This cave was a doorway to and from our world and the enchanted world. So they spent the rest of the day making a hut, fire, and catching some food and fresh water.

"There," said Saphire, exhausted, "we're finally done." They had finished their work and were looking at the night sky. They were also thinking about their family. And for the first time since they left home were sad. They were missing their families. And for this night in the enchanted forest they were safe. But who knows what will happen tomorrow.

During the night it rained very heavily. Their fire and hut was ruined.

"This is all your fault!" yelled Bunny. "If you wouldn't have dragged me out here we wouldn't be lost, hungry and wet."

"Oh I dragged you out here," yelled Saphire.

"Yes," argued Bunny.

"Why don't you just go home," said Saphire.

"I would if I knew where home was," yelled Bunny.

So Bunny and Saphire stormed off in different ways. Will they ever cross paths again? Will our best friends ever talk to each other again? Read to find out.

***

As Bunny headed West she crossed paths with the worst creature ever. A giant hairy Tarantula.

"Oh no," thought Bunny, "what am I supposed to do?"

All of a sudden the spider saw her. Bunny picked up a Y shaped stick, a rubber band (she was wearing on her wrist) and a rock. With these things she made a slingshot. And as the spider attacked her she shot sharp pointy rocks at it. Being very fast and small she was able to dodge its web and go underneath it and confuse it. And finally with a very sharp arrow head she killed it.

"I can't believe I did that," said Bunny.

"Ow!" she yelled and as she looked at her paw she realized she had cut it and it was bleeding. As she wrapped it up in a leaf she walked back to the camp site and hoped Saphire would be there.

***

Now we go back to Saphire, who went to the East. As she walked on she saw this Giant going to eat a helpless deer.

"Let her go," yelled Saphire throwing a twig at his head.

"Huh," said the Giant, "A little thing like you defeating me? Hah! Hah! Hah!"

And for the first time the spot on her belly glowed bright, bright red. And as this happened, the giant took out a club and stared at her.

"You want to mess with someone littler then you. Then mess with me," said Saphire running up and jabbing her spikes in his shin.

Then the giant took a big swing at her. Then with a great leap she cut off his head with a spike on her tail.

"You're my hero," said the deer.

"What is your name?" asked Saphire her spot turning to pink.

"Hi! I'm Hunny," replied the deer. "Can I come with you? I do not want to be alone in these woods."

"Of course," said Saphire.

They headed back to the camp site and found Bunny there.

"I'm so sorry I yelled at you," said Bunny.

"Me too!" said Saphire. And as they shared their stories with their now new friend they rebuilt the hut (now room for 3) and built a roaring fire in a jiffy.

The next day they decided they had to get out of the woods as soon as possible. It was just too dangerous in here. All of a sudden they smelled something. Something DELICIOUS. They followed the smell out of the woods to a little cottage. In there a little old lady was baking cookies, cakes, and lots lots LOTS more sweets. They gingerly knocked on the door not wanting to alarm her. "Oh," she said, stopping her work. "I have some visitors. YaY!" When she opened the door she let them come in and eat as much as possible.

"You little animals are sooooo cute. A deer, a bunny, and a…well I'm not familiar with what you are but you're still adorable."

"I'm a Golopokis," said Saphire. "I'm one of the last of my kind. My family and I are endangered."

"I'm her best friend," said Bunny trying to cheer everyone up.

"This is Hunny," said Saphire.

"Hi. I'm a deer. A giant killed my family. He was about to kill me when this brave young lady saved me," said Hunny, pointing to Saphire.

"You must be tired," said the old lady. "Why don't you stay here and tomorrow you can be on your way home. I have some beds over there. You will get a great night sleep. I know, I've tried them."

As they went to sleep Hunny hurried over to them. "What if this lady is the one from Hansel and Gretel? We will be eaten!"

"No we won't. This lady is nice. Plus her house is not made of candy," said Saphire.

"Now go to sleep," said Bunny.

As they slept the little old lady baked and baked until dawn when she went to sleep. When they woke up the old lady asked them to deliver all the sweets she had baked to the Candy World.

As they headed to the Candy World (with all their load) they got tired.

"Wow," said Hunny exhausted, "I never knew cupcakes and brownies could be this heavy."

As they entered the Candy World they stopped in amazement. Everything, simply everything, was made of candy. Even the people! There was mint chocolate grass, chocolate wood, graham cracker sidewalks, and everyone was made of white, dark, and regular chocolate.

"Wow," they all said in amazement.

"Oh," said the mayor, "the new delivery of sweets is here. Everyone dig in!" And within seconds the whole batch of sweets was gone.

"Thank you so much!" said the mayor. "We were in short supply and the old lady that lives in that house volunteered to bake us some sweets."

"But don't you have some cooks who cook the sweets in your town?" said Bunny.

"Why yes," said a chocolate lady, "but unfortunately they all went on vacation at the same time. We should have planned that better but it was soo short notice and they all wanted to go at once."

"Well," said Bunny, "you have your things now so we'll be off!"

"No," said a little chocolate girl. "You could stay for the night."

"O.K.," said Saphire, "but we'll need food and water and a bed."

"That's fine," said the Mayor.

***

The next morning they said their farewells and were headed in another dimension.

"Let's pick this one," said Saphire.

"Ok," said Hunny and Bunny.

As they went through the dimension they were happy all of a sudden.

"Hello girls," said a little guy, "Welcome to happy land."

Saphire's spot on her belly turned bright bright red.

"Wow," said Saphire in amazement, "I am sooooooooooooooooooooooo happy!"

"If you don't mind," said a little woman, "we just built this amazing amusement park but we are all too small to ride it. We were wondering if you guys would test it out for us. I mean, if you want to. I think it's really cool. Oh, I wish I was just a teensy bit taller."

"Hey," yelled Hunny all of a sudden, "my family had this magic fairy dust. Maybe if we sprinkle it over your town you guys will grow."

"Well," said Bunny excitedly, "let's give it a try."

So all the townspeople gathered in the center of their town. Bunny, Saphire and Hunny took a handful of the dust and threw it in the air. All of a sudden everybody started sneezing. And with every sneeze they grew and grew until they were a regular size.

"Thank you so very much," said a funny looking man. "How can we ever repay you? I know, we will give you these gold medals!"

Then the man pulled out 3 of the shiniest medals of all.

"Wow," they all said with excitement.

"Can we still test the rides?" asked Saphire.

"Surely," said the little old lady.

So everyone got in line for their favorite ride. Saphire rode a huge roller coaster. Bunny rode the bumper cars and Hunny rode the swings. And that day was the best of them all. All of a sudden they saw a little man sitting on a stump crying.

"What is wrong?" asked Hunny.

"The magic didn't work on me. I'm afraid I will just be a small thing no one will notice my whole life long."

"It's ok," said Bunny. "I know we will make you special shoes that can make you go up and down."

So first they took his regular shoes. Then they took 2 springs and tied them to the top. Then they tied the bottom of 2 shoes onto the bottom of the springs. Then they got a scientist to put in something that makes it go up and down by pushing a button. After saying goodbye to everyone they went into another dimension. When they came through they were AMAZED! Thousands upon thousands of golopokises as far as the eye can see. "Oh my gosh," said Saphire, "they do still exist."

"Well, of course we exist," said a male golopokis. "Once they started killing us the rest of us fled to this empty dimension. It wasn't much to look at but we fixed it up. And now it is home. After we were all gone the humans just assumed that we were extinct. But I heard there was one family who still lived there and didn't know about this place. I'm assuming that is you. We were going to get you but we were all too afraid we would be shot by the humans. But you guys found us. Let's see here. There is a golopokis, bunny, and a deer. Well aren't you a strange group of friends. Allow me to introduce myself, my name is Krypton. And welcome home!"

"Wow," said Bunny, "So all this time there were so many golopokises and you never knew about them. And imagine how excited your parents will be. You probably have relatives here."

"Granny," yelled Saphire all of a sudden," My grandmother went missing. We thought the humans shot her. My mother is going to be sooo happy."

"Yes she will," said Granny.

"Granny!" screamed Saphire. "I've missed you so much."

"I've missed you too," said Granny with tears in her eyes. She was so happy that she had recovered her long lost granddaughter.

"Wow," said Bunny, "That is quite a touching story. WOW!"

"But how are we going to get my family here," asked Saphire.

"That's a good question," said Krypton, "for the last (?) years we have been building a transporting device. We have wrote to your family and told them about us. We put the letters through the portal and it comes out the other end. So we know it works. I'll write them now telling them you're here. Bunny your parents also know about this place. They will live here with the golopokises."

"Well, I guess I will just wander around the dimensions looking for a home," said Hunny.

"You won't have to," said a deer coming out of the house.

"Mommy?" asked Hunny.

"Yes," said her mom (Ashley).

"And we are here, too," said her dad (David).

"Katlyn, Jeff, and baby Lilly. You're all here. This is the happiest day of my life. But how is this possible? I saw that giant kill you."

"Well, we were dead but some pixies came along and they sprinkled dust on us and then we were alive. Then we started looking for you. I think it is fate that we wound up in this dimension. With all these nice animals. This is our home, too," said David. At once they got everyone together (by using the portal) and everyone was happy.

"Wait," said Bunny, "we never had Saphire's 10th birthday party."

So everyone had a big party.

The End ☺

Cristansa
= voices heard by group when in a human world

Chapter 1: Isabella

13 year old Isabella Cornaz was just a regular teenager. With brown hair, brown eyes, braces she looked pretty average. She was in high reading and high math so she was considered a geek and a loser.

Isabella and her 3 best friends were very imaginative. They got together every day and just discussed books or ideas for books. Isabella loved witches. She would describe their powers or how they looked. She was a very talented artist so she often drew. She would make them good or bad. The bad ones looked green and had warts and were very old. But the good ones she always made beautiful.[4]

Chapter 2: Katie

Katie was also 13 and a nerd. All 5 of them were in high reading. But only Isabella was in high math. Katie was the one with the most descriptive imagination ever. And she also loved dragons. Katie knew almost everything about dragons. She spent day and night researching them and reading books. If you walked into her room you would be amazed. She had pictures of dragons all over the place. She had ones from all different countries. She also had tons of books on them. But she loved all the classic looking dragons. She was the writer of the group. She was given basic ideas from her friends and she made it into a wonderful story.

Chapter 3: Danny

Danielle, nickname Danny, was a blond hair blue eyed beauty. But surprisingly she still hung out with all the geeks. She was the one who came up with all the ideas. She would make great stories, awesome twists and turns, and the most dazzling endings. All of her story ideas would be different. They would blow away the minds of the group. She would go on the Internet to try and get good ideas of what to write about. She just loved animals. She was a vegetarian and never ever wore fur, or anything that resembled fur. She spent a lot of her time at protests.

Chapter 4: Jasmine

Jasmine was a wonderful red head. She was a very big daydreamer. All through class she got yelled at for not paying attention. In the group she made up the characters. She picked out the names, the gender, their personalities. She sometimes made up animals or mythical creatures that didn't exist. She loved just thinking. Thinking of what they looked like and what powers would go along with their features. She would make up things that would go along with our everyday looking animals. Like dogs with wings and a giant spike on their mood changing tail. Or she would take a turtle and enlarge it to 50 times its size, make it breathe fire and have tentacles for feet.

Chapter 5: The Story

"Ok," said Danny, "let's focus on our next book here."

"Yeah," said Isabella sleepily. Their meetings on Saturday always started at 6:50 am. Isabella was known as a very late sleeper. In fact she almost missed school a few times.

"Let's make this one about witches," pleaded Isabella to the group.

---

[4] Author's note: Add more "drawer" of the group.

"No," said Danny, hearing Isabella's pleas. "I have the most brilliant idea. O.k. guys, there is this place and these creatures. And there in the middle of a war. They are in hiding because the evils and the good people are trying to get them on their side. But they don't want to get in the middle of things. So there is like a leader trying to have everything stay in order. But there are some who oppose the rule of the leader. And they are secretly working for the evil guys. So the rest of them find out and they join the good side to get back at the traitors. Then there is also a big war."

Chapter 6: Their Jobs

The gang met again on Sunday afternoon to see what they were going to do.

"O.K.," said Jasmine as they all gathered in their secret tree house, "let's discuss what all of our jobs are. Isabella and I will work on the characters, and Katie and Danny will work together on the story."

"So we'll meet back here on Wednesday when we're all off," said Katie.

"Yeah," said Isabella.

"So get to work guys," said Danny. "I have to work on a project with that one girl Meagan for science. So I might be a little late."

"It's alright," said Jasmine. "So we're all clear on what we have to do."

"Yes," they all replied simultaneously. Then they said their goodbye's and left.

Chapter 7: Isabella & Jasmine

On Tuesday afternoon, Jasmine and Isabella met up at Jasmine's house. "Let's get started on these characters," said Jasmine getting settled on her bed. "I got some types of characters yesterday and thought they would be good for this book. I thought that they should be animals you know because every book has some animals there."

"Yeah," said Isabella in agreement, "there are animals in a lot of books and they are usually magical or something like that."

"O.K.," said Jasmine, "let's get started. I thought that there should be at least five characters. The first one should be a lion. And he should be the leader of the group. He could have mind reading powers and he can control fire."

As she said all of this Isabella painted a mental picture of the animal in her head. "O.k.," she said after a long pause, "I've got it!"

Then she ran and got her sketchbook and a pencil. She immediately started sketching the lion. After about a ½ hour of work she showed the completed lion to Jasmine with pride.

Jasmine loved it. "This," she said holding it up, "is what is going to make this book great." She gleamed happily. "Now let's get started. We have a lot of work to do."

Chapter 8: The next 4 characters

"So far we've got a lion as a leader but we need 4 more," said Isabella.

"Well I had some ideas of what animals there will be but I don't know the rest," said Jasmine. "Start thinking girl."

Jasmine's 4 characters were a snake, dog, monkey, and an owl. "Just to let you know," said Jasmine out of the blue, "the lion that I told you about is a boy. You know because we have to have some girls in there."

"The first one," she started, "will be a snake. He will also be a boy. He's in charge of defense. His powers can be that he can have control of people's actions and he can also change his size. After that we have a girl dog. She is also in the defense lines. She is just like the opposite of the lion. She is in control of water and she can become invisible."

"O.k.," said Isabella writing all of this down, "this is really good. I'm going to draw them all later but write them down now."

"I'm gonna go on. The next one is a monkey. He's another boy. He's going to be a scientist. He can do many things. He can also fly. And last but not least we have an owl who is a girl. She is an inventor. Her and the monkey were hand in hand on weapons and things that the team needs. Unlike the others she had 3 talents. She has super speed, super strength and she has the amazing ability to time travel."

"But," said Isabella, "do these animals have any names?"

"Oh," said Jasmine, "I completely forgot about the names. The lion will be Kyle, the snake will be Jack, the dog will be Lisa, the monkey Spencer, and the owl will be Maggie."

"Great," said Isabella enthusiastically

Chapter 9: The Signs

Katie and Danny got together at Danny's house for the weekend. They got to work on the story of the new book. Earlier that day Katie got all the notes about the characters from Jasmine. They looked over them now.

"I think it is good," said Danny after reading over them thoroughly. "Yeah," said Katie.

For a while they just sat there and thought.

"O.k.," said Danny, "finally I've got the basic idea of how the story is going to begin. We'll first introduce all of the characters just as they are described from Jasmine's notes."

While she was writing down little footnotes, Katie began typing on her laptop.

"Katie, Danny, thank you so very much for inventing us."

"Did you just hear that?" said Katie.

"Yeah," said Danny looking around. "What do you think it was?"

"I don't really know," said Katie.

"Oh yes you do, Katie," said the voice again.

It was true. In the very back of Katie's mind she had an idea of what it was.

"Let's…take a break," said Danny a little uneasy.

So for the rest of the day Danny and Katie just hung out. And not once did the voice speak again. After they had fallen asleep all 4 of them had very strange dreams.

Chapter 10: Dreams

Katie's dream went like this.

Katie was in a dark forest. Every way she looked she could find no opening. It was hopeless.

"Katie...listen to me." There was the voice again. But this time it seemed very worried and urgent.

"Katie you need to follow me. There is a terrible war going on and you have to help."

"Who are you," Katie shouted. She frantically looked around in all directions, not knowing where the voice was coming from.

She heard something crack – a twig.

"I...I know karate," she lied.

All of a sudden an owl fluttered down from a tree. Katie curiously peered at it.

"Follow me." Then the bird took flight.

"Wait," said Katie, "wait."

She woke up to bright light coming in from the window. "That was strange," she muttered to herself.

Next there was Danny's dream. She had had this dream repeatedly. It was her favorite of all. She was swimming in a shallow lake. The sky was blue, no clouds in sight. Perfect day. Just as she started to relax she heard a voice.

"Danny...Danny can you hear me?"

"Who are you," she said looking around.

"You must come with me. You must help me."

"Come out and let me see who you are," she said trying to act brave.

All of a sudden a snake slithered to the surface of the water. Danny screamed and swam away. Then she woke up. "I hate snakes," she said bitterly.

Jasmine's dream took place on an island. She was deserted there and scared. She ran around frantically searching the skies for some sign of rescue. But no hope. Nothing. She was totally alone. "I'm probably going to die here," she sobbed, sitting down and putting her head between her knees. Then she heard a voice. First faint then it grew louder.

"Jasmine, it's me. You need to come...quickly."

"Where are you?" she asked. "Are you here to rescue me?"

"Come on, hurry." It was speaking very urgently. As if something was wrong. *"A war begins soon."*

"I can't see you," she said looking around, puzzled. "Are you near?"

A dog came out of nowhere. Now this shocked Jasmine a bit. She bent down close and looked at it.

"Hurry...now!" It broke into a run and was off.

Jasmine woke to her sister jumping up and down. "Come on," she pleaded," Wake up and play with me!"

"Settle down," she said, trying to remember her dream as well as she could.

And last there was Isabella's dream. She was in a movie theater. She had fallen asleep during the movie and woke to find no one there.

"Hello?" Her voice echoed off the wall.

"Isabella, now you can hear me."

"Wh…Who's there?" she asked.

"You have to hurry. You need to believe me no matter what."

"I'm not trusting a voice," she said, getting angry. "Come out here now." This was odd for Isabella, giving demands. She was always taking orders and never giving them.

Out popped a monkey. Isabella was so surprised she screamed and ran.

"Wait…I need you."

As she was running through town she noticed nobody was there. She was totally alone. Then a voice called her name.

"Mom," she said, "where are you?"

She woke up to her mom saying it was time for breakfast. "This is unreal," she said looking about.

Chapter 11: The Next Meeting

"I was really freaked out," said Katie after they all had discussed their dreams.

"Me too," said Danny still shaking from seeing the snake, "You know I hate snakes!"

"Did you guys realize something," asked Jasmine.

"No," they all said bluntly.

"Come on it was so obvious," she said.

"Tell us," Isabella said impatiently.

"Don't you see," she began, "Those animals were all in our book. Except…the lion who is the leader."

"That's true," blurted out Katie.

"I remember them saying they needed us," said Danny. "They needed our help."

"We have to help them," said Jasmine," they might be in trouble this very minute."

"What are you all talking about?" said Isabella angrily. "We are talking about fictional characters. I think you are all tired."

"No we're not," said Katie. "You just can't believe. You know it's true but you don't want to accept it."

"Well then you get me some proof, solid proof," said Isabella not knowing what Katie was going to say next.

Everyone was silent. They were watching Isabella and Katie intensely.

"I thought so," she said.

"Then what are we going to do now," asked Danny.

"I think we try to contact them somehow," said Jasmine, searching her head for something useful.

"Well, I'm not taking part in this little silly game," said Isabella, "You can do it without me."

"For all we know, we need all 4 of us to contact them," said Katie, "We need you."

"Oh alright," she said, "but only once."

"So tomorrow after school we'll meet," said Jasmine. "Get some info on how to get in touch with fictional characters."

"Wait," said Danny as everybody was heading out the door. "Why don't we make up a way to get in contact with them. I mean we created them. We're playing God here. Besides, I don't think you can Google summoning fictional characters."

Chapter 12: Magic in the Air

That day at school was pretty normal. All the popular people ignored them. And they lived out their normal repetitive lives. But after school is when they get to their real lives.

Magic was the key here but they had no idea of its presence. They had created a whole world that was in trouble, and now they had to help.

"So how are we going to do this," said Isabella doubtfully.

"Well it's our book so let's think now," said Danny.

"I know," said Jasmine breaking the silence, "We put all our work that we did on the book on the middle of the table." She took all the drawing rough drafts, info and typed papers and placed them on the table.

"Now," she continued, "We turn off the lights." She ran and turned them off.

"My turn," interrupted Katie. "Next we have to put something special of ours on the table with the papers. That way they know it's us."

"Who else could it be," muttered Isabella grumpily. "We're the only lunatics to try this."

"Then," chimed in Danny, ignoring Isabella, "We light a single white candle and put it by the door. So it can ward off trespassers and evil people."

She went and got a candle and lit it carefully, placed it next to the door on her dresser.

"Wait, what about our items?" Isabella took her bracelet off and set it with the papers. "There," she said, happy.

Jasmine untied her ribbon from her hair and set it down. Katie took off her flip flop and put it in. Then Danny took off her mother's necklace and dropped it beside the other's things.

"Are you sure about that Katie," asked Jasmine, eyeing the necklace. "It was your mother's. You don't want anything bad to happen to it."[5]

"It'll be fine," said Danny.

"Now what," asked Isabella, "I don't see anything."

"That's because we're not finished," said Jasmine, "We then get in a circle around the things and hold hands."

They did as she said. "After that," continued Jasmine, "we speak of the place we want to see and the magic word."

"Please," said Isabella sarcastically.

"No," Danny replied, "hope. Hope is the magic word. Hope."

"Hey, hey!" shouted Katie above all the talking, "We haven't named the world yet."

"I know," said Isabella. They looked at her in surprise. "Cristansa."

They all agreed it was a wonderful name for the world. And now the summoning was about to begin.

----

[5] Author's note: More explanation told about Danny's mother's death.

"How do we know what's going to happen," said Jasmine.

"We don't," said Danny.

They took a deep breath and began.

Chapter 13: Cristansa

They spoke Cristansa while holding hands. Then they all said hope (the magic word).

The items on the table emitted an eerie glow. They all watched in silence. Suddenly, like someone was turning off the switch, the items stopped glowing.

They all looked puzzled. It got deathly cold. The girls were breathing hard. Their breath shone white. The candle flicked trying to stay lit. It chilled the girls to their bones. A blue diamond appeared, hovering in the air above their things. It flashed again and again.

Every time it flashed a blue force came out. For the first few flashes it was small. Then it expanded until it engulfed the whole room. The girls just sat there amazed.

A faint voice came from the gem.

"Girls...thank you so much for coming. Jasmine, I thank you for trusting in us and most of all believing."

Hearing her name made Jasmine jump a little, almost letting go of Katie and Isabella's hands. But she had a strange feeling not to because she felt the result of it would be bad. So she held tight.

"Wh...who are you," she said in a shaky voice.

"It's me. Kyle of Cristansa. You are needed so come."

"How," said Danny, getting up enough courage to speak.

"Just let your mind leave your body. In your head you will see me and we will go through the gate. Come now. And welcome to Cristansa."

Chapter 14: The Gate

"O.k.," Danny spoke to everyone, "close your eyes and let your mind go."

They all shut their eyes and concentrated. They felt their minds lift from their human form and go to Cristansa. They landed softly on a pebbled road.[6] They looked around.

"Awesome," yelled Isabella looking around wildly. "We're here. This isn't fake. It isn't a dream."

"No, it's Cristansa," Katie screamed. "We're down there," she said as she pointed to the ground.

It was true. You could see the girls straight through the floor. There they were all sitting in a circle. You could see their breath and their eyes were still closed.

"Well, duh," said Jasmine. "Our bodies couldn't come here. So our minds came. Technically we're still down there."

"Cool," said Danny.

"That's true," said a voice from behind them.

They spun around to see a big beautiful lion with a mane that looked like silk. It had strength yet elegance. It was a wonderful sight.

---

[6] Author's note: More detail

The girls stared dumbly with their mouths open.

"Was it you who was talking through the gem," asked Danny cautiously.

"Yes," said the lion. Its voice was deep and low. Yet it had a hint of kindness and friendship.

"So you sent us our dreams. You're the one who told us to come with you," said Isabella.

"It was I and my companions that sent you that message," as he gestured toward the door.

In strolled 4 other animals. All looking quite unique in their own way.

Katie was the first to recognize the character in her dream. It was the owl. She looked very elegant. Her beak was sharp, talons strong and eyes that shone mysteries and wonders that were her past. She greeted Katie with a polite smile and wave.

Danny saw her person, well animal, also. A chill was sent through her spine when the snake appeared. She had to try all her might not to scream and run. His shiny green and black scales shone in the light. The blood red tongue came from a smiling mouth. But it wasn't a friendly smile. No. It was evil and sinister. As she examined it she noticed the eyes. They were dark and horrible. She felt like she had seen them somewhere before. He greeted Danny with a small bow of the head and a quick wink.

Jasmine saw the dog that had been in her dream. It didn't seem to be just one breed but all of them. She looked like she had extreme power. A stern gaze looked at her. Like it was saying no time to play we have work to do. She was like the lion in some way. Her stance showed she had courage...and lots of it.

Isabella looked at the others. Then at the monkey. People would think that monkeys were silly and crazy but this one had wisdom. Like an old grandfather who had lived 100 years and was dying to get his knowledge out. His tail swung slightly to and fro, which mesmerized Isabella.

"Shall we go in," said Maggie, the owl.

"We shall," said Lisa, the dog. Spencer and Jack led the way.

Untitled #1

Wilted flowers and yellow grass lay at my feet. I walk through the grass towards the decaying tree. Even this far away, I can see it begin to die. I sigh and continue on, leaving death in my wake.

It is a terrible job to kill, it's a terrible life. But it's all I have known, all I have been. Death is viewed as the bad guy and…yeah, I can see where they come from. I take away everything. I am what humans are constantly fighting. I am the eternal end, but a decent guy. I look like your average mortal, as it should be, and I'm a pretty average man, well I guess not man…

Anyhow, here I am, alone. Companionship hasn't always come easy for me, the whole one-touch-and-you'll-be-dead thing is a turn off. Whatever, I can deal with that. It's just…sometimes walking this Earth alone kind of stinks. You may say, "Cheer up, it could be worse." But living forever and killing everything is not much of a life.

And that's why I'm here. After a millennium of searching, "Tandem Hearts Dating Service" has finally found my match. I was younger and eager when I signed up for this. Picture this: a suavely dressed man in his twenties comes strolling in off the street, white suit, shoes, and gloves.

I draw back all my power, but even then, plants brown as I pass by. The building is clean and the people friendly. I walk into the appointment office and sit down on the uncomfortable plastic chairs, waiting. A few minutes later a short fat man comes in breathing heavily.

"Oh boy," he wheezes, "sorry, lunch ran a little late and I had to run to get back. Tim Lesley. How do ya do?"

He sticks his sweaty palm in my direction and I smile politely and shake my head. I didn't want to ruin anything now.

"Hrrm," he clears his throat, withdrawing his hand. "What can I do for ya mister…"

"Dee," I finish for him," Jeremy Dee. Umm…" I can't really find a place to start. "I'm looking for someone to spend the rest of my life with."

"Yes, I had figured that much. Well if you fill out this sheet we will get you into the computers right away."

I took the papers that were slid towards me. I glanced at the pages. 10 pages of information! Dang! Don't these people know I have a job. A rather…demanding job. I got up with a smile.

"I'll get these mailed to you ASAP. I have to get going…pressing matters to attend to." I hid my wry smile behind a cough. I'm the only one that ever gets my jokes, such a shame.

"It's been nice Mister Dee. I'll hopefully see you soon."

I checked my watch and turned to the door.

"I'm sure I'll be seeing you very soon, sir. Now good day."

10 years later I was surprised when I got the call and rushed back to this small Kentucky town right away.

***

I remember looking at the list for the first time. Lounging against a tree I opened up the laminated folder. It yellowed against my gloved hand, but I didn't mind; I was sort of used to it by now. I absentmindedly ran my now bare hand over the tree trunk. I cursed and jerked it away but the damage was done. I jumped away as the tree began to decay and decompose right before my eyes.

Sighing I began to walk, still reading the questions. The first one had me thinking immediately.

What are you looking for in a woman?

Hmm…initial thoughts: pulse, doesn't mind hanging around graveyards, good personality. I think I'll put that last one down.

It took me awhile but eventually I got down to the last question.

What do you want to do before you die?

That last question sitting at the bottom of the page made me pause. It made me think. So here's a little information about me: I can never die. Never.

Now this small fact made this last question a bit confusing. I just took it as this: What do you want that you can never have?

I knew what I wanted. I wanted sunlight with blooming flowers. I wanted sweet kisses and laughter. I wanted children and pets and a house in the country. So…what did I want to do before I died? I wanted to live.

Allie in Forks, WA 2009

Untitled #2

My eyes drift away, unfocused and unclear. The sounds of the room muffle within seconds. I can feel the drugs taking over my body. I have no idea what they gave me, and right now, I really don't care.

My limbs feel funny and tingly. I start to giggle. What's so funny? I think, dazed. Nothing. Nothing about this is funny. But I'm still giggling. And I can't help it.

Have you ever taken a risk? Jumped off the high dive? You get a certain feeling. Indescribable and fleeing in its nature. You're left with such a rush that you can't think straight. All right then. You know what I'm talking about. Now…have you ever taken drugs? I know what you're thinking. "Who? Me? No way. I'm a good person. Not some druggie." Yeah well that's what everyone thought, what I believed. But let me tell you a bit of a fact. Bad people don't take drugs, the drugs take a good person and turn them bad.

I was a regular kid. Ok, maybe not regular. Honestly…I was a nerd. Plain and simple. Average guy at a below average school. Public school, I shudder at the thought. Hi, I'm Cameron. And before you start to label me, I think you need to hear what I have to say. I'm not pleading innocence. No, it's nothing like that. I'm warning others, when you're faced with this, run. Don't think you're strong enough, because you will never be. No, I plead ignorance over innocence. So ignorant in the ways drugs can alter your life so much, that you don't know which way is up. So come along and I'll show you my journey down the rabbit hole. Please don't wander off now. It's very easy to get lose in Wonderland. Very very easy.

"Just do it, little wimp."

Yes, ladies and gentlemen, that is where it all started, at the local swimming pool when I was 8 years old. The high dive was in front of me, menacing as ever. I took a tentative step forward. I'd never been this high, I didn't know people could get this high. Clouds floated by below me and birds cried out tauntingly. Well…that's what I imagined. Now I just think it's funny, how scared I was to take that first jump. I wasn't even that hesitant with my first time of using. But back then I didn't know what would happen. I was sure I would die, but letting my friend Tom have bragging rights over me was not acceptable. I looked down and inched a little further. The tips of my toes slid forward, dangling. Deep breathin', squeeze eyes shut tight, and jump.

***

My heart thundered as the wind howled around me. I gasped and my eyes opened, surprisingly right in front of a wall of water. I smacked the surface and my body twisted and turned underwater. I surfaced, sneezing the water out of my nose.

"Haha," Tom smiled, "fun right?"

I took a deep breath and nodded, amazed. That freedom felt right. It felt good.

Tom grabbed onto my wrist, "Come on, let's do it again." He towed me along, grinning all the way.

Actually, Tom was the one that introduced me to this mess. He opened the door to a little drug called crystal meth. I wouldn't call him my dealer; perhaps my provider. In any sense, Tom gave me what I wanted. Now, I'll start telling you about that night.

I grabbed the handle of the door with quiet eagerness. I breathed and calmed my nerves. The door swung open before me. Red eyes looked back through a hazed of smoke. She was sitting on the couch alone, needle in hand. Of course she would be here, nowhere else she'd be on a Tuesday afternoon.

"Cam," she smiled, "come sit. I've missed you."

"Isabelle, please…you have to come home." I pushed the needle away, disgusted.

But was I hallucinating or did my hand shake? I hadn't been this close in a long while. I could feel the slight pinch at the crease in my elbow, the pinch…then release.

I wasn't that bad in the beginning, of course. Just because I jumped off the high dive at 8 didn't mean I was a druggie the next day. No, it took time. A couple years of breaking curfew, shoplifting, etc., to let the temptation worm its way to the center of my mind. Even then I was scared. But that's where that feeling came from. Knowing its wrong but learning that it feels damn right.

I digress. I was about 15 when I first tried weed. Greatest night if I can recall. Well, not until I saw the beauty of other temptations. But I just have to explain myself. It wasn't that I didn't know the dangers. I did. It wasn't that I didn't know what would happen to me if I got caught. I did. It was that curiosity. That fucking curiosity that makes you wonder where that damn rabbit went. It makes you peek into that rabbit hole and look into the dark world below. You think you're stable, you think you have your balance, so you lean further, just a little. Then the world slips out of view and you're falling.

Senior year I met Isabelle. Beauty in black. Tall, blonde and goth. But I guess I liked that. Don't ask me now, I guess it was a phase. She had transferred from the city and had oozed newness. I could smell it on her, or that may have been the drugs. I'm not so certain. The agitation in school and hazy eyes after were a sign, I guess. I probably knew it all along, though. Like

I knew all along that she would be the downfall of me. But like a good little boy I followed her, my evil little Cheshire cat.

***

She glared at me.

"What the fuck? You think you're too good for me just because you've sobered up?" She got to her feet, wobbling to the fridge.

"I don't need you around anymore, Cam. Jack gives me everything I need."

That was a blow. And I could see I'd given some of my anger away from the look on her face. She smirked and I glared.

"Jack's a pimp, plain and simple. And you're being used, Isabelle."

She grabbed my face in her hands and kissed me. Fiercely forcing my guard down, stripping my defenses away.

"Come on, come back to me," she whispered to me, sliding the needle into my hand. My breathing labored, I looked down. I smiled slowly.

But Isabelle had a charm to her. She was cute, funny, so in control that you didn't even know it. Her first week here she had already picked me as a target. Sidling up close in English class she laughed at my lame jokes, touched my arm and whispered sweet things to me.

"Want to get high?"

I smiled devilishly at this girl by my side. Her being female, I would have said yes to anything. The drugs were an added bonus. Walking out of class, I followed close behind her, ogling in every way she wanted me to. Mr. Turner put out a hand just before I was out the door.

"Cameron, your grades have been slipping. Please, can you tell me what's wrong?"

I looked into the hall at Isabelle at her locker. She looked up from her conversation to wink at me.

"Not a goddamn thing."

***

I had already given into her the moment I turned that door handle. Three months of sobriety were thrown out the window. The only thing I was conscious of was the here, Isabelle at my side and meth flowing through my veins. Then after that things got blurry, hazy, smoky. A few days later I came back to reality.

***

"We need to run away, Cam." Isabelle was already high when I got to the party. "This shit town isn't enough for us. Tom and some people are driving to Vegas…and I'm going, too."

Nowadays I was pretty easygoing, but this grounded me, at least for a moment.

"But…what are you going to do in Vegas?"

"Tom knows a guy, Jack, I think." We're gonna get into business out there. It's gonna be great. But I need you, Cam. Come with me."

For 18 year old me, this seemed like a hell of an idea. I grinned, genuinely pumped. "Okay, what do you need from me?"

***

Saturday I woke up entangled in sheets. Where the fuck was I? The last 3 days were a drug filled montage of insanity. It was 8:00 at night and I was in Isabelle's bed. Way to fall off the wagon, Cam.

Isabelle walked into the room wearing her "work" clothes. She had dyed her hair a bright red and went by the name Ruby on the streets. "Time to party, baby."

I followed my red queen out the door. I knew I was breaking my morals, but right now I didn't give a shit. I needed to get high.

Money was what they needed from me.

Allie, age 15, North Beach, Oahu, Hawaii

Blood Moon

It…it's happening again. I can feel it. My senses heightened. Fur growing all over. A thirst…for human blood. I stepped off the back porch and howled at the moon. Yes, I was becoming a werewolf. But not just any werewolf, a super werewolf. I guess I should start from the beginning.

Two weeks ago it all happened.[7] My name is Margret Jena Bleemy. But all my friends call me Maggie. I am 15 years old and I am a freshman. Yes two weeks ago I noticed a few "changes" happening to me. But this wasn't just normal puberty. It was something so much more. It was a regular Saturday night and I was at a sleepover. Her name is Karen and she is my best friend. It was 7:00 and she decided we needed snacks so we both walked to the nearest gas station. That was when I didn't feel so hot.

I was walking along when it hit me. The most intoxicating smell of my life. I turned to Karen and asked, "Do you smell that?"

She looked at me puzzled. "Smell what?"

That moment she turned to me a new wave of the smell came over me. I looked at her. "Did you get a new perfume or something?"

"No," she said, "what's wrong?"

"It's just you smell soooo good, like steak or something, but sweeter."

By then we had just arrived at the store. We walked in and headed straight for the candy aisle.

---

[7] Author's note: add description

"Well, I didn't do anything different," she claimed.

I inhaled the sweet mouthwatering smell again. I heard my stomach growl and said, "Come on, I'm starving, let's get stuff to eat."

We shuffled down the aisle, grabbing things that looked good, when all of a sudden a man walked in. He was wearing a black hoodie with the hood up so we couldn't see his face. He had his hands stuffed into his pocket and his head was on the floor. He walked to the counter and stood in line.

I kept my eye on him as we made our way to the counter to pay. When it was his turn at the counter he stepped forward and pulled a gun out. Karen screamed and hit the floor.

"Put the money in the bag," he told the clerk, shoving a duffle bag at him.

I still hadn't reacted yet so, I was just standing frozen to the spot with my mouth open. The man turned to me and said, "Get down on the floor before I blow your brains out."

"Maggie," Karen whispered, "get down. Please do what he says."

I stood there scared stiff. Karen grabbed my arm and pulled me down…hard. The clerk handed the now full duffle bag to the man and then ducked back under the counter. The man took a look around and then headed for the door.

Just then the clerk emerged with a shotgun. He fired 2 shots at the man as he was running out the door. One grazed his arm and the man cried out but kept running.

Right after he was hit I smelled an incredible smell. Without thinking I ran after the man, running at my full force to catch up. He didn't see me as he headed into the dark and deserted park.

I hid behind a tree and watched him. I felt strange inside me, hungry. A hunger like no other. I knew if I didn't eat something soon something bad would happen. And somehow I knew that something bad was gonna happen soon and it would involve me and the robber.

I felt a pain in my mouth. I reached up and touched my teeth. For some reason, two of them felt…sharp. I opened my mouth wide and enjoyed the growth of my teeth. For some reason they felt like they belonged and were part of me. I was starving, ravenous and now I knew what for. I knew what I had become…a vampire. But I didn't care about anything now except the robber nursing his wound on the park bench.

The smell of his blood was too much for me so I approached him. I must imagine I looked like a cat stalking pretty, ready to leap and rip the throat out of its victim. The robber was surprised and immediately drew his gun. But when he saw who it was he chuckled to himself and set the gun down.

"You come to arrest me, little girl?" he said, examining his wound.

I stalked closer to him looking him over, deciding which way to attach.

"Get lost bitch," he growled, "before I shoot you."

I quickly jumped over to him. He got startled and smacked me across the face. I turned back to him with a smile. Blood was dripping down my chin. I wiped it with my finger and stuck it in my mouth. It tasted odd but sweet.

I turned to the man and smiled.

He got scared and ran away. I chased after him, gaining up in seconds. With amazing strength, I tackled and pinned him to the ground. At first he tried to fight back but realized it was useless. Instead he tried to cry out for help.

"It's no use," I hissed, "you're dead now bitch."

But the strange thing was that I wasn't me saying those things. Well, it was me, but it was a whole different part of me. A part that wanted to kill.

I opened my mouth and bit into his neck. He screamed with pain but it didn't faze me, I kept on drinking. The sweet warm flow of blood going down my throat and into my stomach made me feel renewed. I felt whole and good.

I laid the man down once I drained him. I got up and turned to leave when I saw someone behind me. Karen stood there open mouthed gaping at me. Since I wasn't hungry anymore I felt like myself again.

"I...I can explain," I stammered.

"Okay," she said, "you explain. I'm going to throw up in those bushes right now." She laughed shakily and headed off towards the nearest bushes.

"Karen," I called, running after her. "I'm just...don't...I mean...you...I...gosh."

"So," she turned to me, "you're a vampire. How long have you known and not told me?"

"I swear I just found out today." I stopped a few feet away holding up my hands to show her I wouldn't hurt her.

"Oh Maggie," she cried and ran over to me and hugged me fiercely.

"Uh, Karen, remember I'm still a vampire and I can smell your blood," I said to her.

"Oh." She removed her death grip on me and stepped a few feet away.

Untitled #3

Jamie looked around her in disbelief. *This can't be happening. This is wrong.* Jamie Ann Range has always kept her cool in very tough situations. This is exactly what she prided herself on. She had to figure a way out of this mess. This couldn't be happening; it just wasn't logical.

Jamie had always lived in the reality of things and she grew up pretty fast for a fourteen and a half year old. After her father had been sentenced to life in prison when he accidentally shot and killed a bank teller in the process of the robbery, child services really got on her mother's back.

"Mrs. Range, do you realize how much stress city life can put on a young girl?" The weasely looking man threw a glance at Jamie who sat on the couch trying to appear inconspicuous.

Liz seemed tired as she mustered up a smile for Jamie. "Yes I suppose you are right Mr. Neil. Jamie needs a change in her life, a fresh start."

Liz's expression suddenly changed, looking on into space. "This city is holding her back from her dreams. She needs to be free."

"What?!" Jamie leaped off the couch and gaped at her mother ignoring Mr. Neil's look of disgust.

"Teenagers," he mumbled, "always making things difficult."

"You can't expect me to uproot my life so you can live your dreams!"

"Jamie, please, we will discuss this later," her mom pleaded with her.

"Fine, I am going out! I will come back around dinner."

As she headed out the door, she heard Mr. Neil whisper to Liz, "I blame the father; bad genes."

She spun around and fixed him with one of her coldest stares (she had been working on this in the mirror and was proud to say it was coming along nicely). She was satisfied to see him flinch away as if she was going to hurt him.

Two blocks away Jamie stopped at the big iron gate. It may be kind of creepy to other people but Jamie loved going to the graveyard to sit and watch the sunset.

Other people didn't usually hang around with Jamie because they thought she was strange. She was considered a nerd among her fellow schoolmates. With her long brown hair and glasses she looked like a younger version of her mother, which unnerved her a bit. The only thing different about her was her turquoise eyes that people always complemented her on. Her secluded silence usually drove people away due to the uncomfortable silences that were frequently in the conversations. But Jamie did not mind this one bit. She liked the solitary feeling of being alone and longed for the sanctuary of the library during the boring hours of school. Yes, she enjoyed being alone with just her thoughts as company; she was an outsider in a world where everyone belonged.

She hopped the fence because, of course, adults thought kids would try to break into the cemetery. How insulting.

When Jamie had an issue she usually went and talked with her grandmother. Her grandmother was a sweet and gentle woman that loved everyone, or so Jamie had heard. Her grandmother died when Jamie was six years old in a faulty surgery.

Sitting down Jamie replaced the flowers by the head stone. "Loving mother and grandmother. Yeah that was you. I don't want to leave you here alone." Jamie wiped a tear away from her eye in frustration. *Stay strong. Don't show weakness. I can do this. Time to grow up.*

***

Jamie slowly got out of the car. The house her mom had shown her looked more appealing online. The old cottage over looked a huge lake. The glimmering water reflected the sunset beautifully. Contrasting to the beautiful scenery, the broken down fence running along the outer region of the house and the gravel driveway looked very tacky.

"Jamie, I am going to unpack," called her mom from somewhere behind the boxes in the car. "You can go wander."

Sighing Jamie looked around. *Oh joy. Where to start?*

Jamie went around the side of the house where there was a short wooden dock jutting out into the lake. "I wonder if I would be a boat girl." Jamie wondered aloud.

"I don't know. You don't look like you can handle the sea."

Jamie turned to see a tall boy standing at the edge of the woods. "Hi, my name is Kyle. I live around here."

Jamie barely registered this, she was too busy staring at those honey brown eyes that melted you to the core. Kyle looked like one of those guys who were tall and thin but had muscles that were unseen. His hair was so fair it looked like it was white and his ears seemed to come to a point. Perfect teeth peeked behind full pink lips. Jamie instantly lost her cool and swooned over this lovely being before her.

He walked over to her. "Want to go swimming?"

"Uh. Well," was all Jamie managed to get out before she heard her mother calling for her. "I'm sorry. I have to go, but if you would like come over for dinner it would be great."

"Actually I can't, but I can meet you here tomorrow. Alone." Kyle fixed her with a serious stare. Jamie felt a chill run down her spine. Dismissing this as nonsense she turned to him.

"Sure," Jamie replied watching him run off.

***

Jamie opened her eyes to a gray, dusky sky. She moaned and rolled over. Growing up in the city, Jamie was used to minimal sunlight. Getting out of bed she looked around. Walking over to the window she pulled back the soft white curtains. She had to admit to herself that even though she hated moving, inside she felt as if she belonged here, in the wilderness.

Out of the corner of Jamie's eye she saw a shadow. Turning she examined it more closely. Kyle stood at the dock; eyes closed staring into the sunlight. Wearing only his swimming trunks his bronze skin glistened in the sunlight. *He must love the wilderness, committing himself to waking up early in the morning. I wish I was like that.* With gracefulness that Jamie couldn't even manage, Kyle dove into the lake. Emerging from the lake Kyle shook off his hair and stood up. Jamie jumped when she looked at him.

Where his normal honey brown eyes had been were black pits of darkness. His skin no longer glistened but stood out pale and greenish against the back of his swimsuit. Long black nails emerged from his hands and feet. He stared back at Jamie, completely aware of her staring back. Slowly, an evil smile crept across his face. Sharp, jagged, yellow teeth that looked like they could tear the flesh from your bones snapped at her. A shimmering wet fin jutting out of his head slowly molded back into his head. Within seconds he was back to the boy she had met a day ago. Everything had gone back to normal, except his eyes, which glowed with intense passion and rage.

She let out a little yelp and shut the curtains. Running downstairs she flung herself outside in her shorts and a tank top. The sharp stones cutting into her feet hardly bothered her as she raced to the dock. Halting and gasping for breath she looked around in despair.

He's gone. Where did he go? What is he? Sinking to her knees she put her head between her hands. *Am I going crazy? I know what I saw but no one will believe me. Think logically; this does not happen every day. This is not real. This isn't reality.* Reluctantly she got to her feet and headed inside.

"Oh, I'm glad you're dressed. We are spending the day with some of the neighbors," her mother called as she walked into the kitchen. Dressed in shorts and a t-shirt, sweat was already dripping down her back.

"Mom?" Her mother half turned from making sandwiches. "Do you believe in fantasy? I mean do you believe that things in those books I read can come true?"

"What are you talking about, dear? You know those things are just fantasy. I know moving is stressful for a person, but things will get better."

"No, mom," she complained, "you don't understand. I am not stressing. There is this boy and…well he is not a normal boy." But it was obvious her mother could not hear her. Jamie let out a big sigh and stomped up stairs.

Throwing her laptop open she logged onto the internet. *I have to find something on them. I am sure he is one of them. From all the books I have read he matches the description exactly.* After about twenty minutes of searching through mindless dribble she finally came across something interesting that could pertain to her situation.

The traditional water dwelling nymph usually lives near large bodies of water; the mischievous nymph may try to lure innocent mortals into the water by using numerous methods. Once into the water they will try and drag you down into their kingdom until you drown. Once dead you are of no use to them and they will release your body, allowing it to float back to the surface. Some of them may take on human form for the daylight hours and prey on young maidens living within the area. But once dusks hits they must return to their original form and retreat into the water again. Jamie closed her laptop slowly. Thinking she hardly responded when her mom called her name from the bottom of the steps. *It all makes sense. Why he wouldn't come to dinner and at dawn when I saw him in his true form.*

"Jamie did you hear me calling you?" Her mother's voice shook her out of her trance. "The neighbors are here, please help me move the food outside by the bonfire."

For a minute Jamie was scared that Kyle would be at her house waiting for her, but looking out the window she relaxed. The moon shone full in the sky and darkness cloaked the wilderness surrounding her. *I'm safe at night. But how long can this last?*

The night wore on around her, and people slowly dispersed. At the end of the night she was thoroughly exhausted. Her mother walked inside to clean off the dishes. Gathering the garbage from the tables she heard a faint tune flittering through the air. Dropping the cups on the grass she slowly walked toward the music.

It was a soft melody that seemed to surround her and go deep within her soul. The music entered into her body and went deep into her soul, pushing all her worries away from her heart. Her body ached if she stood still and her legs burned to move. Walking forward she faintly realized that she was walking to the lake. Her mind was fuzzy but she knew something was wrong. Whenever she tried to form coherent thoughts in her mind they were pushed away with a blast of the sweet, enchanting, enriching music. Her smile faded from her lips and turned into a grimace as she willed her body to halt. The pain of immobility was no longer an ache but a full-fledged pain, bringing tears to her eyes. *This can't be happening! This is wrong!*

All around her things remained the same but she was caught in a battle for her life. The noise of the woods echoed in her hollow mind and the fireflies swarmed through the air, swaying in time with the music. Swarms of fireflies flew around her face landing on her nose and cheeks. Stopping she shooed them away.

I stopped! The fireflies, they did something to me!

She looked around her in a daze. What she took to be fireflies were little fairy creatures landing on her half extended arms twittering away at her. Amazed Jamie fell to her knees and lifted one of the fairies to her face. Their light blue skin stretched taught over very distinct bones. They were nothing that Jamie had ever thought fairies to be. Tiny little teeth poked out of their mouths and their giant black eyes with thin membranes slid over them frequently. The translucent wings attached to their back flittered away in time with their chattering.

They are trying to tell me something. They helped me. They...they saved my life.

A fairy flew up to her face making her jump. Pointing and flying in circles the fairy's twitter turned into a squeal of fright. Tearing her eyes away from the fairy she turned her head and looked behind her.

A black shadow engulfed her and she felt extreme pain all over her body. She screamed and crumpled to the ground curling into a ball. Blackness and despair filled her mind and warm tears slid over her cheeks. Pain, hopeless heavy black pain, all over her body and deep within her soul, reaching every corner of her existing self. A white light flashed before her eyes and everything went black. Before she was unconscious an uninvited presence entered her mind. *Sleep my dark princess. You will awake and fulfill your destiny…*

Jamie awoke to an intense pain in her head. She stumbled up and looked at her surroundings. She was in a dark cave by the lake. It was nestled in the trees on a nearby mountain. Glancing through the trees Jamie saw the gleam of the lake shining in the dense forest. Taking out her now destroyed phone she examined her face.

Blood trickled out her ear and down her neck. Her eyes had a strange glow to them. Normally her eyes got darker at night but in the moonlight they seemed to gleam green. Her long brown hair was matted at one side. Quickly she pulled it into a bun and out of her face. Her hand froze around her ear. Running her fingers over it she examined a newly formed point at the top of her ear. She gasped. Turning around she looked at her skin. The same pale sight greeted her. Opening her mouth she looked into the screen. Two fine, sinister looking fangs protruded past the edge of her top lip. *What did that thing do to me?!*

She quickly rushed out of the cave. Turning around the bend she ran into something hard. Looking up from her bleeding arm, now gouged by a rock, she saw a face that made her insides turn to ice.

Kyle's handsome face stared back at her. In the early morning light she could still see the tint of his green-like skin. Quickly she examined herself again for any strange coloring of the skin.

"No. The royals don't change colors. But you will find yourself pale and your hair turning black."

"What about these other changes?!" she yelled jumping up. "My eyes and ears! What did you do to me?!"

"Relax," Kyle replied grabbing her arm and towing her to the cave. "Last night those wretched little swinglings removed your glamour. This is what you truly look like. Even you could not see through the glamour the dark lord provided you."

Jamie sat down, tears streaming down her face. "Please, change me back and let me go home. I am just a girl. I don't want to do this anymore."

"You don't know do you?" Kyle settled down against the wall opposite of her. "It all happened about fourteen years ago." Not wanting to listen to Kyle, but intrigued by his voice she lifted her head.

"About fourteen years ago the dark lord met a young and beautiful nymph. Hair as black as night and eyes that bore deep into your soul. He instantly fell in love with her and had a secretive affair. Nine months later she bore a beautiful baby girl, the only heir to the lord's throne. The lady of the dark, Nalia, soon found out about this abomination and demanded it be thrown into a river of fire. Cloaking a baby calf as the child the ceremony was gone through with while the actual baby was switched in place of a human child." He paused and looked at Jamie closely in the face. His eyes held a sense of security and sincerity in them. Mixed with the passion of his voice Jamie was spellbound.

"Tell me, Jasmine, for that is your true name, have you ever seen things that you thought might not be real. That couldn't be possible. Well they are real, and one day you will reign over them with an iron fist."

"How...how do you know about all this, Kyle?" Getting up he walked over to her. Standing over her he looked menacing in the gray early light. "My name is not Kyle. It is Kashta, and I am to be your husband."

***

Jasmine walked up to the bed in the dimly lit room. Looking down at her mother's sleeping form, Jasmine gently touched her cheek. Jasmine knelt beside the bed slipping the note under her mother's pillow. Kissing her face, she rushed out of the house, biting her fist to stifle her sobs. Kashta gazed at her from behind the broken down fence. It was no use running, he would catch her and it would all end up the same.

Jasmine walked down the narrow bridge with Kashta holding her arm so tightly she could feel the bruises start to form. "It is time to fulfill your destiny Jasmine. It is time to go home."

Tears streaming down her face, Jasmine threw a glance back at her new home, her real home. Her mother lay asleep in her bed, boxes lying around the house. *Mom will be up soon. I should have left a note. I wonder if she ever felt that I was not her baby. That I was some kind of monster.* Disgrace entered her heart and she turned around. She did not deserve the life she was given. *Time to grow up and move on. Time to live your life.*

Stopping at the end of the dock she looked down into the liquid black water. At dusk Kashta told her it was time to make her journey into the other realm...the fairy realm. Jasmine knew it was useless pleading with him and felt she should go with him.

Everyone should know about their heritage and where they came from. If her mother ever found out what she was then she would not want her anyways.

Jasmine thought back to her letter. Her last form of communication to her mother; at least for now.

Dear Mom,

I can't explain this to you and I know you will be confused, but I had to leave. Ever since I was young I have seen things. I hid it all from you from fear of rejection. Oh how I wanted to be perfect in your eyes. But I know now that I can never be perfect for you, because I was never yours. I can't explain it all to you because he is waiting, waiting to take me away. Just know that I have loved you all my life and will always love you, even if you will not return my love. Why I have to leave? I cannot say.

"It is time. Jump Jasmine, jump to your destiny." Kashta's voice made Jasmine jump out of her day dream. Taking a deep breath Jasmine closed her eyes on the world she knew. The world that nurtured her and befriended her in her times of needs. With one simple step she plunged herself into the black unknown water of her future. *Who knows,* she thought as she was falling, *maybe I can rule the fairy world well. I can be a great ruler who brings peace to the whole kingdom. My destiny has been laid out for me...now it is my chance to follow it.*

Untitled #4

The door flew open and a dark moss engulfed me. Struggling I escaped and ran for my life. Down the ancient stairs, I bolted, ignoring the groaning cry they let out. I hurtled through the front door and slammed into something hard and solid. I looked up from the floor at my best friend. Kevin had recently hit a growth spurt and looked adorable in his blue jeans and sweatshirt.

"Thanks," I growled as he lifted me to my feet with one hand.

"Did you see that," I nervously asked glancing behind me. "Come on, we need to run! I think it's coming back." I felt a chill to my bones and was running in seconds.

Kevin stopped me as I ran away from the old house. Breathing hard we sat down in the middle of the forest.

"What was that all about Kara! I have been looking for you – "

"Shhh!" I whispered harshly.

"I don't hear anything."

"Exactly," I said standing up. The forest was still. Silence all around us.

"It's coming. We have to move. Now!" But I already knew it was too late. A trance was going over me. My vision blurred and the world spun under me. Through the haze I could faintly see Kevin lying next to me unconscious. When I woke up I was in a whole other world. Creatures I have never seen before whizzed by on wings or crawled to the slimy mud and muck that coated the floors.

"Welcome to the last door on the right," a small goblin came up and greeted us. His teeth were yellow and rotted and his gnarled hands rested on the small hilt of the sword at his hip.

"Where am I?" I said quietly shivering. I knew that feeling, the thing that was chasing us was here.

"No one is supposed to go into the house," the goblin continued ignoring my questions. "You and your friend will meet with the king to decide your fate. You're lucky if it were me IT would have gotten you."

All of a sudden I was grabbed from behind and blindfolded.

"Come on," the goblin growled, "the master doesn't like to wait."

I had a faint feeling we were inside because the darkness was overwhelming me. Pitch black all around. I tried to reach out for someone, for anyone. The air chilled and I fell to the floor weeping. The blindfold was ripped from my face and there lay Kevin. Even though I wanted to run to him I knew I shouldn't move. I don't even think I could move. The presence before me had me rooted to the spot, fear traveling through my whole body. Inching toward Kevin's unconscious form and grabbed his hand, waiting for my punishment.

A smile broke across Kevin's face. "Happy Halloween, Kara."

Confused I looked around. The strange creatures behind me were beginning to look like poorly dressed classmates. Lights flashed on, blinding me.

"You...did...this," I stammered, angry beyond coherence.

"I had to pay you back," Kevin laughed, tears streaming down his face.

Fuming I got up from the ground wiping my own tears of fright from my cheeks.

"That wasn't funny."

"But its Halloween, Kara. You got me last year so I returned the favor," Kevin explained becoming more serious.

"Oh I understand, Kevin," I said looking him in the eye. "I understand that you got me and I will get you too. I will get you back and you'll never even know it was me. It will leave you begging for your mommy."

For a second Kevin's eyes gave away the fear he felt. Then he crossed his muscular arms and regained his composure, "Go ahead. Try it."

I skipped home happy of scaring Kevin and happy it was all over. The year of my fourteenth birthday and I had survived. In two hours' time my birthday party would start and it would be the best I had ever had. Some people think that being born on Halloween is a bad thing. But I enjoy it, I relish in the dark and frightening. Just maybe not as scary as what just happened. But I had survived the terror of Kevin. And soon it would be my turn to unleash terror.

Walking into my house I was greeted by lively music and all my friends. The strobe lights flashed and they all yelled "Surprise!"

A smile crossed my face and I jumped into the crowd conversing with all my friends. Within moments I abandoned all forms of conversation and danced, letting the music flow through me, rocking my body on its own accord.

"Does this make up for scaring you?" Kevin screamed over the music dancing next to me.

"Maybe," I replied giving him a sly glance and jumped right into dancing again.

"Hey mom, can Kevin spend the night?" I called after the party had died down. Since Kevin and I had grown up my mother didn't care if we spent the night together. "As long as Kevin sleeps in the living room."

"Come on, Kevin, let's practice our body in karate moves for the competition next week."

Going to the garage we found our old boards piled up next to the car. Breaking the wood made me feel alive and invincible. But before long we were both tired out.

"Goodnight Kevin," I smiled at him, leaning and kissing him on the cheek. "Thanks for making this my best birthday ever."

I leave Kevin standing at the bottom of the staircase holding his hand to his cheek with a bewildered expression on his face.

"See," I called to him, "I got you too."

Rebecca Kline

Park Forest, Illinois. A house in the distance noisily bustles with people of every age. We see a girl chasing after two older boys. No matter how strong and tough those boys look, it is no match for the fearsome determination of young Rebecca Kline. She weaves in and out of yards, intent on catching her two older brothers, Nate and Neal. Falling and scraping her knee does not stop her. No, Rebecca is far too used to injury such as this.

A young girl, barely four years old, is taken to the hospital for stitches when she smashed her head on a fish tank. Mother and father, Natalie and David, anxiously wait to hear if their daughter is ok. Whether it is getting hit in the face with a golf club or bit in the eye by a dog, Rebecca Kline has always come out on top with more than one story to tell. With siblings Neal, Nate, Ritchie and Sabrina already starting their lives, Rebecca awaits her turn to leave the next. This young active girl has a mind for sports, music and cars. But her dreams can change it all.

A vision of a little house with possible kids, a job at St. James hospital and a happy life in Illinois is all Rebecca is hoping for. But can the fun loving little girl take on the responsibilities ahead?

The road to maturity is a long one that all will have to travel one day. At age 8, Rebecca lost her uncle and in 5th grade the loss of her grandparents started her maturing process. Now at 16, she is still her "outdoorsy" self, making close friendships with Erika, Kristi and Jeff and enjoying being a teenager. But she has set her mind to her future as a pediatrician. One piece of advice she would like to let her younger self know is "Treasure your education more and think before you act. Just live life every day at a time."

Now an adolescent, Rebecca has hopes for a bright future ahead and has the mind to accomplish it.

Untitled #5

"What have I gotten myself into."

Eighteen year old Candice Johnson climbed through the window, dropping onto the cold dark floor in the cellar. Candy was certainly hanging out with the wrong crowd lately. She sighed, thinking of what her mother would say if she could see her now. Spikey blond hair stuck out at all angles, the downside of being your own hairstylist. Her green eyes shown through the darkness. But she had left the lectures behind, the lectures and the rest of her family. In Minnesota, her mother was definitely by now up at the local bar. Three years ago the newspapers had a party when "tragically an eleven year old boy dies from a hit and run." Oh how much she hated those damned newspapers. Her little brother Nate would have snickered at her attire now, but that was the past.

"Candy! What are you waiting for!?" a voice harshly whispered from the yard. "Hurry up!"

Glaring out the window, shadowy figures moved away from her. *They will get what they deserve; they always do*, thought Candy to herself. How did she get to be here when just 3 years ago there had been high school, dreams, and that boy? Oh Dylan Howard had been the evil she just couldn't get away from, and frankly didn't want to. He was the one who convinced her to join him in Boston. And where was he now? Dead, face down in the alley out back. Who killed him? Well that is where Candy came in on this whole scheme.

***

Candy was not necessarily good at goodbyes. So when Dylan knocked on her bedroom window, she just left. Pitching her old cell phone in the driveway, Dylan slipped the razor into her pocket.

Cinderella
From the view of Anastasia

Of course of course! Everything has to be about her! She gets her name in every story book across the country and who do people know me as...The Ugly Stepsister! How dare them! I have feelings you know. As some of you know by now my name is Anastasia, stepsister to Miss Perfect. Now you all might pity the sweet blonde servant girl but I will tell you now that it is wrong. No one got the real true story of how Cinderella was just a whiney, evil girl who ruined my life.

At first I was excited to meet my sweet new stepsister. How wrong I was about that. I admit I was jealous of Cinderella at first. Those curly blonde locks, perfect teeth, sea-blue eyes, I mean, what girl wouldn't be. But when I met her I knew how horrible she really was. She was a brat as a little girl and she tortured me. But who would believe her. Miss Perfect could do no wrong. When her father died I thought she would have changed. She did change, I found out later, she changed for the worse. She was infinitely paranoid that my stepmother was going to steal the fortune that her father had left her. This is when things got crazy.

In the spring many people would visit our estate, especially the reporters for the newspaper. One day we were having an especially public and formal gathering. Cinderella emerged dressed in rags that were a bit too revealing.

"Cinderella," I pleaded with her, "please put your nice clothes on and throw that thing away."

I just want to point out that in no way did I command her to clean my clothes or do my hair or any other chores.

"No, Anastasia," she cried out above the noise in a pitiful voice.

Great! The girl can act above everything else…I'm screwed.

"Please don't make me scrub the floors. I am so tired from trying to do your makeup and waxing your back."

You see what I mean! What lies she had told to our guests. Just to make us look bad.

As you might as well know by the end of the night people had a different image of us. So that is how the whole evil stepsister thing got started. We were pretty much hated throughout the village and Cinderella kept up her act whenever someone was over. If no one was over she sat on the couch stuffing her face with food and commanding us to do her work.

"Fetch me this, Anastasia. I want that Anastasia."

Oh how I wanted to cut off all that pretty blonde hair, but I couldn't. No, then she would have proof that we were the evil ones. I would just have to wait.

Her little act got so creative that she actually started talking to mice. Mice! Talk about mad, but she did it for the public. The only way my family was going to redeem its honor was to make an excellent appearance at the ball and tell the truth to the prince. We made sure Cinderella did not suspect us leaving. We carefully snuck out and proceeded to the ball. I had a lovely talk with the prince and I was sure he was going to dance with me. All of a sudden Cinderella emerged in a beautiful gown. My little prince was love-struck and spent the rest of the night with Miss Perfect.

I learned later that Cinderella made up some story with a pumpkin and fairy godmother to explain her amazing appearance. What she really did was tear apart my dresses to make a beautiful gown while my room lay in wreckage. She and the Prince went to his room and at twelve she fled the castle. I am not sure why she did, but I heard she left more than a shoe behind.

So I am sure you know the rest. The Prince searched for Cinderella and they got married. A week later, guess what. A bouncing baby boy emerged to the public. What a surprise, right? I lost contact with Cinderella and had a family myself. Today she spends her days eating chocolate and getting fat while Princey is off doing who knows what. I have never shaken off the name Ugly Stepsister but at least I have my dignity.

"Boyfriend" Love

"Why are you doing this, Shannon?" Mike lay on my couch flipping through an old magazine.

"Shut up!" I yelled throwing things out of my closet and onto my bed.

"I can't find my black dress," I sighed falling to the floor.

"You don't need to do speed dating. You are perfectly fine and you can find a date the normal way." Getting off the couch he leaned against the frame of my door.

"Mike you don't understand. I am desperate now. I need a relationship. I am a twenty year old woman living in New York, alone. I need to find someone. And this can help."

"You don't need to go look for someone when he is right in front of you," Mike whispered under his breath.

"And like I told you before, it will ruin our friendship," I replied crossing over to him.

His black curly hair and big brown eyes made my heart warm. But it would never work out between us, too much history.

"I think I'm falling in love with you Shannon, and I don't know how to stop."

He leaned into me and closed his eyes. One hand slipped around my waist and tugged me forward.

Skipping out of his arms I left him at the doorway in mid kiss.

"Blue or red," I gestured at the two dresses lying on the floor.

"Blue," he smiled at me.

***

Twenty minutes later I was standing before my bedroom mirror. The silky blue dress went to my knees showing my pale long legs. My blonde hair lay in curls flowing down my back. *That's not gonna last*, I thought, recalling my too straight hair. Mike's head popped into view.

"You are going to be late." He gestured to his watch.

Grabbing my purse, I took a deep breath and headed out the door.

***

I entered the drafty restaurant, glancing at the small tables with a cheesy flower center. As the night commenced, the desperate creatures of speed dating emerged. From the old man chewing tobacco to the Spock impersonator, I was feeling down within the first few minutes.

Through the night I met the most interesting people.

Towards the end of the night my last contestant stepped forward.

"Ben!"

"Oh my. Shannon what are you doing here?" My ex-boyfriend eased himself into his chair. His green eyes sparkled behind his glasses and his hand nervously ran through his red hair.

"I thought you were dating Liz," I questions, feeling overly exposed in my short blue dress.

"I am. I am just here to help my friend." He pointed three seats ahead of us to a balding sweaty man. "He was nervous so I said I would do this with him, but why are you here?

"Oh you know just…looking." I nervously averted my gaze from his face. He left me broken hearted for my best friend, how can he still make me giddy.

"I would love to catch up sometime. Liz can't get out a lot with her being pregnant."

I gaped at him, tears forming in my eyes.

"We are expecting twins," he grinned, "isn't that wonderful?"

"Um…yeah, great. Will you excuse me, I think I left…my…um…shower on, and I really should turn it off."

I scrambled from my seat, unaware of the stares. I bolted for the door, the tears already pouring down my face, leaving messy mascara streaks in their wake. The empty parking lot echoed my footsteps and muffled sobs.

"How could she be pregnant!" I yelled to no one in particular. "I hope their baby is ugly," I muttered, stepping into my car and slamming the door.

***

"Hey I came as quickly as I could." Mike stepped through the door and shook his wet tousled hair.

"Did you bring it," I sniffled trying to see through watering eyes.

"Double chocolate chunk," he smiled holding up an ice cream container.

"Ugh, thank goodness!" I cried bolting for the tub of ice cream.

"Whoa! Nearly took my hand off there, Shannon."

"Sorry," I apologized around a mouth full of ice cream.

"So what's wrong? You sounded really distressed on the phone." He pulled a chair close to me. With gentle fingers that slightly shook he moved my tousled, ratted hair out of my eyes.

"She's pregnant," I sniffled.

"Oh, how could he!?!"

"Even when we're apart he still manages to hurt me."[8]

"He is a jerk," Mike consoled me, "he doesn't realize what he let go. You are an angel and you are too good for him."

Always like Mike to put it in perspective when all I really want him to do is go pound the crap out of Ben.

"I know, I know. I just wish I could make him feel like I did. Like I do."

"You should be thanking him, Shannon."

I blasted him with a fiery look, willing him to burst into flames.

"Hey, don't give me that look, let me explain before you rip my head off. Maybe he felt like you were too good to stay with him. So he did what he thought was right, he broke your heart in order to let you go."

I glared at him. "You wouldn't know anything about this!"

---

[8] Author's notes: Protagonist – Shannon & Mike. Antagonist – Ben. Dynamic character – Shannon. Characterization dialogue.

"Really, Shannon," his voice shook. "I think I would because I can't let you go and god have I been trying to!" He waved his hands over his head in an exasperated gesture.

"You think I haven't tried to move on, tried to find love with someone else. I can't. And do you know why I can't?" he whispered angrily, moving close to my face. "I think the reason I can't let you go is because you won't let me. You keep me close because you don't want me to leave you. But you are too scared to open your heart to me."

He took a deep breath, standing and heading towards the door. Halfway out the door he paused and turned toward me with glistening eyes.

"What you don't see is you have already given your heart to me. And I to you, the first time I saw you I knew you had stolen my heart. Now it is just time for you to wake up and realize that we were meant to be together."

He walked out and closed the door gently behind him. I curled on the couch too upset with myself to do anything else. *Why do you take him for granted so much*, I gently scolded myself. *He was right. You need him.*

"I need him," I whispered out loud, my voice slightly cracking. "I need him," I said louder.

I jumped up, nearly falling over my dog Sammy. Sammy looked up at me with curious eyes.

"Sammy, I love him." I smiled, bending down to kiss his muzzle.

"I need him," I whispered, throwing my coat over my wrinkled dress and headed out the door. Running back inside, I quickly checked my makeup, then confidently strode outside to meet my soul mate.

***

Mike stood in the pouring rain, waiting for a cab. *She will never speak to me again*, he thought glumly. *Well, I can get along fine without her.* He climbed into the cab, reciting his address to the strange looking cab driver with an eye patch. He can remember the first moment he met her.

***

How they met…

Mike careened down the hallway of his university, catching fly away papers as he ran. The empty school echoed his heavy breathing and thumping footsteps back at him. Running, he glanced to his side, seeing the room he was destined for fly by. He quickly halted, throwing already disorganized papers across the floor. Grabbing them, he stood and threw open the door. Apparently the door was lighter than any door ought to be. After banging dreadfully loud against the wall, the door swung back and smashed into his face. His consciousness wavered, but through the blur he could see all faces turned toward him. Sensing the eyes, he tried to convey his awareness to them by taking a step forward and immediately buckling to the floor.

He awoke later to the sunlight streaming in from a window. He got up and stretched his back stiff from lying on the cot in the nurse's office.

"Oh boy did you get smashed in the face. It was like a split second and then BAM! You're on the floor bleeding from your nose."

Mike turned to the tall blonde girl sitting across from him. Her grey eyes twinkled with laughter and she gave off a slight cinnamon scent. *Did I die?* Mike asked himself. *I must be unconscious because a girl like this does not exist.*

She came over and sat by him. "Shannon Livings, nurse's assistant. You're lucky I was here and not Mrs. Taylor. Ugh," she shuddered, "you would not do well waking up to that."

"Uhh, thanks. Mike Nelson." He sat next to her and offered his hand. After a moment she took it, shoving him on his back.

She laughed at his confused expression and explained, "Get some rest, Mikey. You look like you need it."

He closed his eyes, not falling asleep for fear of forgetting her, his petite little heroine. But she was there when he woke up and for 2 years after that he was helpless against falling for her.

***

Mike saw her even through the dirty cab window and the passing rain.

"Of course," he said with a slight smile, "she never told me the shortcut she had found to my apartment." He stepped out of the cab and paid the driver before turning to look at her. Shivering wet she still looked beautiful. Her dress was plastered to her legs and her coat was drenched. A smile lit up her face when she saw him.

"You're right you know," she said slowly walking over to him. "I don't want to let you go, and I'm not going to any time soon."

Mike smiled, leaning closer to her. "You have put me through hell, you know."

"Aw, you're a big tough guy." Shannon playfully punched him on the arm. "I think you will live."

He bent down to kiss her, stopping close to her mouth. The rain streamed over his eyes, causing him to close them. "Are you sure you want to do this?"

"Oh shut up and kiss me!" she cried, grabbing his neck and pulling him forward. He pulled away and led her to the door.

"I think this is the beginning of something great."

"Yeah, I can rub it in Brad's face," Shannon said evilly.

Mike stopped and stared at her.

"Just kidding!" she cried, running for the door.

Mike sighed and chased after her, a grin on his face.

The Midnight Story[9]

Once upon a time there was a man named Mark. Mark had a family. He had a daughter, son and a lovely wife. Their names were Amy, Jake and Lisa. One day Lisa was washing the dishes when Mark came in.

"Honey we need to talk," he said. "I want a bigger home. The bottom line is that I want to move."

"O.K. We'll start right away," said Lisa.

The next day they told the kids.

"What we're moving! I can't move," yelled Amy.

"It's fine with me," said Jake.

So a month later they started packing.

"Where are we moving to anyway," said Amy.

"WolfSide Hill," said Lisa.

"That sounds creepy," said Jake.

A week later the moving van had got there and they were all set to go.

"O.K. Everyone buckle up," said Mark.

And with that they were off to WolfSide Hill.

---

[9] Editor's note: It's clear from the handwriting, spelling and development of this story that Allie was young when she wrote it. Her interest in fantasy and suspense comes through even in these early stories.

WolfSide Hill was the spookiest place Amy had ever been. "I don't like this place," said Amy.

"Yah, it gives me the creeps," said Jake.

The van pulled up to a big old house. You could barely see it because it was so dark. The family moved up to the front porch. Lisa was about to open the door when it swung open. Jake and Mark jumped. Amy and Lisa screamed.

"Wow, that was a little scare wasn't it?" asked Mark.

"Yah," answered the family. Just then a dog came running at them. It was a golden retriever.

"Hi, little fellow," said Jake.

"Can we keep him?" asked Amy.

"Of course, what do you want to call him?" asked Lisa.

"Bubbles," said Jake and Amy together.

After that the family started going through their things.

"O.K. Your mother and I will go in this room. Amy you could have that room and Jake you could have that room," said Mark.

Mark, Lisa and Bubbles settled into their room. It was a big room with windows. And it had one bathroom in the back. The bathroom had a big bathtub with one sink. It had two mirrors in it.

Jake's room was big also. He had his own bathroom. There were 3 windows in his room. In his bathroom there was one window, one sink and one shower. There was no bathtub. Jake loved his room.

Amy's room was the biggest. It had 4 windows. She also had a bathroom. It had two windows. It had a shower and 1 bathtub and it had a big sink.

When they were all settled in they went to bed. It took a while for Amy to fall asleep. But when she woke up it was morning time.

"Amy! Time for breakfast," yelled Lisa.

"O.K. Mom," yelled Amy back.

Today's breakfast was eggs, bacon, milk and cereal. Afterwards Jake and Amy went outside to play. The neighborhood was not so great. There was garbage everywhere and there were no kids in their neighborhood.

"I hate this," said Amy.

"It's ok," said Jake.

Untitled #6

Have you ever wanted to take your own life? Ever wanted to throw away the special gift that you were given? It is a curious thing to think humans want to end their lives prematurely when I have given them such short of a time here. How precious they are, how weak but beautiful in their simplicity. Ignorant yet constantly learning.

The only thing you can rely on them to do is change, alter, in a perspective so unique that I myself crave the change. I yearn to see the end in sight so that I might soak up my world and everything in it.

But no, there is no end in sight for me. No way to stop, no one to comfort me. Throughout time it seems that everything must come to an end sometime right? Everything must eventually stop?

Not in any way have I seen proof of that. So why do they constantly kill? It is because they can never know how wonderful it is to breathe when the next breath might be your last.

They can never know the constant torment of time, real time, not years but an inconceivable amount of time that really cannot be explained. Unless you have lived it.

No, they can never know this…and that is why they are happy. I think I have stopped feeling for myself now, I only live through them. I grant them with life and they grant me with feeling something so special even the agony or losing the ones I care for feels wonderful. Because to just feel, that is what makes a life worthwhile.

¿Loved or Lost?[10]

I agree with the statement that it is better to have loved and lost, then to have never loved at all. I think that, as humans, we need to take chances and risks in order to feel any emotion at all. I think that even if we do feel that pain when we fail or lose love that we once had, we will have experienced something that, as humans, we will eventually experience.

It is in our nature to feel love and pain because it shows us that we are capable of feeling strong emotions for something that was. To have never loved at all means that we can't know, experience or feel that love that will cause such a reaction that shows us that we cared for something so greatly that it was able to hurt us so deep.

I think once we realize that we are human and that we benefit from these lost loves, that we grow and mature with each experience, we will be better inclined to take those risks and chances to be able to feel something great.

---

[10] From Allie's class journal

Untitled #7[11]

Once upon a time there were three hikers. As they were walking along hiker #3 slaked behind. He got split up from the group.

As he was walking he noticed he was lost so he sat down.

All of a sudden he hears this growling. It happened in a snap. A wolf pops out of noweare [sic] and starts biteing [sic] his arm.

When he wakes up he is at camp. It was all just a dream, thought number 3. But then he looked at his arm and he saw the bites.

He told his fellow campers all about his insodent [sic] in the woods. They thought he was nuts. Then he showed them the bites. They said he should see a doctor about the bites.

The only person in the woods was this Jepsey [sic]. She said these bites came from a wearwolf [sic]. She also said that at the full moon tonight you will become a wearwolf. The only way to stop it is if you die.

They walked back to the campsite thinking about what the Jepsey said. They ignored her and that night #3 started to transform into a WEARWOLF!

He chased his friends to the brige [sic]. When his back was turned they pushed him off the bridge and he died.

The End

---

[11] Editor's note: This is another one of Allie's early stories, age 10

Clumsy Puppy[12]

One January day in Washington, my father and I decided it was time to get another dog. Walking into the shelter the smell hit me like a baseball bat to the face. No matter how much I love and care for animals, no human can get used to the smell of about 30 newborn puppies.

Overcome with excitement, and a little dizzy from the fumes, I rushed to the cages, picking up the puppies and nuzzling them. Getting stares from some others in the room, I regained my composure and walked back over to my dad. Looking back at the puppies, I could see one out of place, wary of humans yet as playful as any newborn should be. Abandoned in the shelter's parking lot had put these pups through a lot.

Picking up the little dog I held him in my arms and knew that this would be my puppy.

Loading him into the car we soon discovered a surprising fact. Did you ever know dogs can get carsick? Me either. One stop at the gas station and a new pair of pants later, we were off to the house.

The hardest thing we discovered in that week was potty training the now wild pup. Running him out into the yard is hard enough without it being in mid-pee. But it was worth it to see this cumbersome little dog review his new surroundings.

One day, seeing my stepmom's other dog jump up on the couch, Goliath had in mind he could accomplish it. Backing up, he had a fierce look in his eye. He paused, and stumbled on, getting his front paws on the couch

---

[12] Editor's note: Clumsy Puppy is a true story about Allie's "Washington Dog," Goliath, joining the family in 2009. Allie frequently visited her dad, stepmom Ruth, stepbrothers Toby and Kai and of course, Goliath, at their home in Bellingham, Washington.

and the rest of him off. Tumbling on his back he got up and shook himself off. A smile seemingly on his face he walked toward me. Picking up the little puppy, I placed him on the couch, next to me, his body stretched out across mine.

Minutes later Goliath returned to his natural playful self. Getting up and stretching, he overestimated the width of the couch and backed straight off. Once again wounding his dignity, he strutted off not looking back.

Months later, this cumbersome little pup is a lot bigger, but still is as playful as always. A water loving dog, Goliath now spends his time swimming at the local dog park and blowing bubbles with his nose. No matter how hard it is to raise a puppy, it all is worth it in the end.

Allie & Goliath
Summer 2011
Lake Padden, Bellingham WA

Untitled #8

In a vastly flat land I found several huts clustered around each other. With interconnecting roads and pathways, their village seemed civilized. Walking up to the entranceway, I saw the organized trees and bushes, decorating the front area. The inhabitants of this hom sweep hom appear to be in competition with the other residents of the area. Whichever hut transforms their area into the biggest spectacle, gains respect from the others in the area.

Walking into the humble hut, I shockingly take in my surroundings. On the walls, mutilated animals hang, their blank eyes staring into space. These dead and desecrated animals warn intruders to stay away from this hut. A painted sheet of canvas is plastered to the wall, of a pot of flowers. These hangings are then worshipped by the inhabitants of this house. Lighted sticks sit at the corners of the room, illuminating the entire room. I walked into the middle of the room, noticing the strange tradition of placing one's footwear by the door. This symbolizes the inhabitants desire to keep the house "clean."

A section of cloth lies over the hard wooden floor. This signifies the center of the room. Box-like objects are positioned around the chairs. Many of these types of people will sit on these cushioned objects and spend hours in this room, every day of the week. In this same room, a wooden case holds figurines. These figurines are on display to the entire room, and are worshipped by the people who live in and enter the house on a day-to-day basis.

The main focus of this room is the magic box that sits on the wall. Big and black, it hangs above my head in the center of this room. With one wave of the magic wand, the box lights up and emits a series of sounds and images. The inhabitants will sit in the room and receive all of their information from their magic box. This box is also a sign of wealth and status among these peculiar people. The bigger your box and the more boxes you own raise your status. It is a ritual that the whole family takes part in, watching their magic box every day. They are a type of people always needing to be informed.

On the opposite wall there are drawings of the inhabitants for all to see. These are displayed to any guests or intruders that may enter the house. The inhabitants bare their teeth to show their dominance over their domain and their power. When guests or intruders enter, they will be intimidated by these ritualistic drawings and have more respect for the inhabitants dwelling in this house.

These simplistic creatures have a gaping hole in the front of their hut. With this hole, they can not only let in light, they can also see the outside world. Meager amounts of cloth are placed over this hole. I assume their purpose is to disguise themselves and their home. Whether or not they know that this is no way of protection is still not apparent.

What is apparent is that these strange inhabitants use this room primarily. They partake in ritualistic events that strengthen the family ties within the clan. Fiercely protective, this simple race of people will go to great lengths to ensure that their hut is not intruded upon. How these hut-dwelling inhabitants live among each other is a mystery. They care only for themselves and their own kin. Another obvious fact is that these creatures are always in competition with each other, displaying their magic machines in front of their house for the rest of the village to see. What is found in the rest of the hut is still unobserved, but I have no doubt that it will lead to further understanding of these creatures.

Untitled #9

Darling,

All my love. How I wish we were together again. It seems like, so recently, I was holding you. You guided my life and my choices. Without you I am lost.

Now that you're gone, life is so quiet. How did we lose each other?

Last night, we were on the couch, comfortable and safe. Now, I look around and am lost. I search for you every day. I will go to the ends of the earth for you. My life is so dull without you near. I stand in my living room and utter a heartbroken cry,

"Where is the remote?!?"

Untitled #10

Twinkle twinkle, little star, how I wonder what you are.

My mom always used to sing this to me before bed. Curled up I dreamed of stars. So far away from me, taunting, dancing, beautiful in the mind of a 5 year old. When I woke I would grab my notebook and try to draw a star. Crooked, blue, and with 6 points, it wasn't very realistic, but it was something. And I was proud.

At ten mom moved out. Left me, daddy, and a world of questions.

"She just needs a break. Once she feels better, she'll come back."

Every morning daddy would say this to me over my Captain Crunch. That would be my morning routine. Wake up, feed Jojo, "She'll come back one day."

In high school it was a little more than depressing. Dad was tired, I could see it in his eyes. Tired but finally accepting reality. Sure, we had discussions about mom, like before. But I could tell his energy was just gone. He was reciting words from memory, without really meaning them. But it was ok. We both knew how to deal with it, and we both moved along. My graduation was soon to come. I was finally thinking about the future. Where was I going? What was I going to do?[13] I accepted one night that I would stay and look after my father, go to junior college, and just live life.

At dinner one night, I could sense a strange feeling in the room. The knowledge every teenager will acquire, when the time is right. There was

---

[13] Author's insertion: dad has accident

going to be a discussion tonight. A real discussion. Not routine talking, it was different.

Look what I found," my dad looked at me as I was putting dinner in from of him. Was it just the light or did he look older, his hair more gray, his wrinkles more pronounced? I peeked over his shoulder to look at the drawing in front of him. A crooked blue star stared up at me. My mouth drew up at the sides with the memory. Smiling, I sat down.

"Honey, I know you think I need you to watch me, but if I am holding you back from your dreams, then I can never be happy with my life." He paused and looked me in the eyes.

"I got you this."

He slid the pamphlet across the table to me. Bright colors and smiling faces looked back at me. I looked at him, uncomprehending.

"I want you to go there. It's the best nursing school in New York. I know you'll love it."

"Daddy," I choked out. "I have always wanted this. But...no can we afford it."

He blushed. "I have been saving and borrowing. Don't worry hun, you're all set." He reached over and wiped my tears away.

The dazzling lights, the people, the smells, sounds, everything. This was New York! And I was finally getting my chance to live it. My plane set down at 2 am. Exhausted I climbed into the cab and headed to my new apartment. I thought of my dad as I was falling asleep on the hard floor. I would never forget what an opportunity he had given me.

"Caleb Jivens." That's what he told me as we got on the subway.

Volcanoes

Once upon a time there was a great and powerful fire goddess named Toran. She lived happily in the heavens with her three children Archer, Weava, and Fortune. None of these beings possessed any powers except for Fortune. Her two powers were being able to control fire, like her mother, and being able to tell the Future.

One day Fortune had a vision. She saw the god Peroser, lord of the sea, coming to destroy them and take the command over Earth. She suggested that they kill Peroser now so he won't get the chance to kill them.

But Toran wouldn't listen because she doubted her daughter's abilities. She said Peroser would never do anything to hurt them or upset the balance of power. She also told Fortune that if she tried to hurt Peroser she would stop her no matter what.

So with the help of her brother and sister they managed to lock Toran up inside the Earth. After that was done they went and took care of Peroser. In the battle Weava died but eventually they killed Peroser.

Toran, locked up inside her prison, was furious. She took all her fire power and pushed upward. This created a mountain. Again and again, Toran did this until finally the Earth broke open and lava poured out. But despite her effort she could not escape.

So from time to time Toran takes her anger out on the Earth. She vows to someday break free and get her revenge.

Enchanted Island of the Time Heart

It was still dawn when Saphire came out of her cave. Her and her family were the last of the dragons. Her kind had been hunted and drove into hiding long ago by the humans. How inferior they looked scurrying around in their metal death traps, living at the summit of a never before seen mountain had its advantages. No being hunted by fleshy little men and their small but terrifying metal sticks. What a world this had become. How Saphire longed to be free, flying with the wind beneath her powerful blue wings. But no. Her father has warned her more than once they had to be discreet. Sighing, Saphire ducked back into her cave awaiting her family to be awakened.

***

"Get away from it!"

"Ha ha ha, look at the little baby. You actually believe in dragons and fairies. What a loser."

Jerry Lewis came up close to Vicky's face.

"I think that's hot," he whispered for only her to hear. Quickly he kissed her on the cheek and threw her book at her.

"Come on guys, she is not worth wasting our time on."

Vicky stood rooted to the spot. Jerry was her arch nemesis like Lex Luther to Superman. But maybe underneath it all he actually liked her.

That's nonsense, she told herself, *he was just messing with your head*. Besides he wouldn't go for the geeky smart ass. Vicky gathered up her books and headed for home.

Man's Best Friend

"Wow," exclaimed Sara, "our tree house is awesome!"

Sara Linn and her best friend Christina Manson were building a tree house in Christina's backyard. Sara and Christina had known each other forever. Both their moms went to college together. Sara and Chrissy (Christina's nickname) were 12. Chrissy was only 3 days older than Sara but she bragged about it like it was a year.

"This is going to be great," said Chrissy. "An all-girl tree house and no <u>Vicky</u>."

Vicky was a very mean girl at their school. She was a teacher's pet, show off and she thinks she is the boss of you.

"I don't even think she cares," said Sara.

"Oh! She will, she will. And when she wants to come up I'm gonna say no you can't come up," screamed Chrissy. "You knocked my books down in 4th grade. So now you must suffer. Ha Ha HA!"

Sara stared at Chrissy. "You have to stop doing that," she said, "you're freaking out the whole neighborhood. Including me."

All of a sudden their puppies came to see them. Both of their mom's dogs had puppies. They only kept one. Sara got a mischievous little puppy named Demon. Demon was a husky.

Chrissy had an adorable lab named Lilly. Lilly and Demon were like best friends. They always played together.

Sara and Chrissy went down the ladder to greet their dogs.

"Hi Demon!" screamed Sara and swept her little dog off his feet.

Lilly, Demon, Sara and Chrissy went to Sara's house for lunch.

***

"What do you girls want to eat," said Sara's mom.

"TACO BELL!!!" the girls shouted.

"Oh no, I'm not going out," Sara's mom protested. "Plus it's starting to rain."

"The tools, blueprints and everything are outside," cried Chrissy.

The girls ran outside. With the dogs. Then they saw a huge mud puddle. The dogs immediately jumped in. Rolling, splashing and fighting. The girls decided to jump in, too. They wrestled with each other and their dogs having a blast.

Suddenly Sara thought of their stuff. She darted off to the tree house. Seeing her reminded Chrissy of the stuff also. The dogs soon followed the girls to Chrissy's backyard and to the tree house. They picked up their puppies. The ladder was slippery but they managed to get up, except for a few occasions where they almost slipped.

Once they got to the top they found their stuff. But it wasn't that wet. Now, they didn't finish the railing. So when Chrissy went to lean on the railing she fell out of the tree to the ground with Lilly in her arms.

When Sara saw that she ran over. While running she slipped and fell off the tree house. Both of them lay on the ground in the rain unconscious.

When they woke up they were in Sara's room.

"Oh thank god they're up," said Chrissy's mom.

Both their moms rushed in to Chrissy's room to check on their daughters.

"Mom, how did we get here," said Sara.

"Chrissy's mom saw you two out there and called me, "said Sara's mom in relief that her daughter was awake. "Together we brought you in."

"You two stay here," said Chrissy's mom. "The doctor will be here shortly."

"Mom!" complained Chrissy, "We're fine. We don't need a doctor."

But just then the doorbell rang.

"Well speak of the devil," said Sara.

As their moms went to greet the doctor and tell him what happened, the girls heard something.

"Man, falling out of a tree was great," said a tiny voice.

"Thank goodness we landed on Sara and Chrissy," said another voice.

"I hope they're okay," said the second voice.

Huh thought Chrissy and Sara.

"Did…did you just hear someone talking," stammered Chrissy.

"Yah," said Sara.

They looked around and nobody was there. Then their eyes fell on the puppies. Sara looked at Chris as if asking "did those dogs just talk!"

"No, no," said Chrissy, "It couldn't be."

"Hey. Hey why are they looking at us?" asked Demon.

"Oh my gosh," exclaimed Lilly, "I...I think they can understand us."

Sara and Chrissy just stared at the dogs wondering if they were going crazy. They saw the dogs' mouths moving but words, actual words, were coming out of it.

"Wow," said Sara after a long silence.

"Great," said Chrissy, "We were geeks before but now we're the crazy people."

"I think it's kind of cool," said Sara. "Should we tell anybody," Sara asked.

"Are you kidding, we'll be in strait jackets before you can say 'kokako'," yelled Chrissy.

"Cool," squeaked Demon.

"We're the first dogs to communicate with humans. We could go down in history like Santa or George Bush or even Lassie," said Lilly.

"WOW!" they both daydreamed about what it would be like to be famous.

Demon jumped up and looked at Sara.

"Hello...How-are-you," he said slowly.

"We're not stupid," said Chrissy to the little husky, "we are just AMAZED!"

"So," said Lilly also jumping up on the bed, "what exactly is a shoe?"

"What?" said Sara. "Um...a thing we wear on our feet so we don't step on things."

"Oh!" said the dogs together.

"I have a question," yelled Demon, "What are those things coming out of your paw?"

Chrissy and Sara looked at their hands.

"We don't have paws," said Chrissy, "they're called hands and the things coming out of them are called fingers."

"Wow," said the dogs.

"We have a question for you," said Sara.

"Yeah," said Chrissy, "Um…what should we ask them," she whispered to Sara.

They both thought for a moment.

"Oh, I got one," said Sara all of a sudden. "What do you guys do when were at school?"

They looked at the puppies with interest. The dogs looked at each other like saying are those two stupid.

"We just, you know, play and sleep and stuff," said Lilly.

"Oh," said Chrissy.

"So," said Sara, "What do you guys want to do?"

"I have an idea," said Chrissy with an evil smile on her face.

"I don't have a good feeling about this," said Lilly.

"Me either," said Sara.

"Cool!" said Demon.

"Oh guys, listen up," Chrissy said, "Vicky always goes to the mall today at 4:00. So we go to the mall and go to her favorite shop."

"Abercrombie," said Sara. "Then we have our dogs attack her. Oh yeah while we put Sharpie® on her face and hair."

"Wow!" said Demon, "I'm so totally in!

"I don't know," said Lilly, "is this a bad thing to do?"

"No," said Sara explaining to the little dog, "Vicky is very mean to us. So she deserves this."

"Oh," said Lilly happily. "Let's get her!

***

At 4:00 they had their mom drop them off at the mall. As they walked in they hid their dogs in their backpacks.

"Ready?" said Sara.

"Ready," said Chrissy.

"Ready," said two little voices in their backpacks.

As they walked into Abercrombie they saw her. When she saw them she smiled a vicious little grin.

"Oh hello freaks," said Vicky, "What do you want Linn and Manson?"

"Oh nothing," said Chrissy.

"You two are too geeky for this place, said Vicky, "plus why are you wearing backpacks at the mall. Gosh! Why do I bother asking you losers."

"Here's your answer," said Sara.

Just then their two dogs came out and tackled her to the ground.

"Gross! Ewww! Get your drooly little mutts off of me," screamed Vicky.

The dogs pinned down her arms as Sara and Christy drew all over her face. It said loser and stupid, freak, all kinds of stuff. Finally they let her up.

"Oh you two will pay for this," she screamed, "you'll be dead at school."

"Yes!" said Chrissy.

"We did it," said Sara giving Chrissy a hi-five.

"That you both. That was really fun," said Lilly.

"And plus she totally deserved it," Demon said. "I loved seeing that look on her face when I licked it."

As Vicky hid behind a trash can she watched them pick up their dogs and start talking to them.

"Oh I've got you now," she said. Then ran away to the parking lot.

"We so got her," said Chrissy.

"Oh yeah," said Sara in agreement.

That night they had a slumber party. With popcorn, hot fudge sundaes, marshmallows and a whole lot of movies. That night they were stuffed to the point of vomiting. The next morning they spent the whole day walking and playing outside with their puppies!

"You guys are so cool," said Chrissy throwing a Frisbee and having Demon catch it.

"Wow, I've had so much fun with you guys I can't believe we've never bonded like this before," chimed in Sara as she fed Lilly little dog bones.

"We should be getting home," said Chrissy, noticing it was starting to get dark. "Yeah and tomorrow is Monday."

So they made their way home and said goodbye. In the morning they walked to school together.

"I really wish we could have brought Demon and Lilly," said Sara sighing and thinking of them.

"I hope nothing bad happens to them while we're gone," said Chrissy with a worried look on her face. "What if someone takes them."

"Don't worry," said Sara, reassuring her. "They will be fine."

As they walked into school everybody stopped talking and stared at them. As they looked around they spotted Vicky looking at them with her marker colored face.

"Why aren't they making fun of her face," Sara said to Chrissy.

"I have no idea," whispered Chrissy and looking like she was going to punch somebody.

"Hey Crazies, are you going to talk to dogs," said a boy with bright red hair.

"What…what are you talking about," said Sara looking very confused.

Just then her friend came up to her.

"Sara," said her friend Jenny, "is it true you guys talk to your dogs?"

"No," said Chrissy, "why? Did someone say that to you?"

"Well, yeah, Vicky is spreading the word that at the mall yesterday, she saw you to talking to your puppies," said Jenny. "You know after you two attacked her."

"She didn't," said Sara.

"She wouldn't," said Chrissy.

"Oh I'm going to kill her!" yelled Sara.

No normally Sara doesn't do this. But she is outraged with Vicky. Chrissy would have gone to beat her up but she is the sensible one now in this situation.

"Oh, it's you," said Vicky seeing Sara coming at her.

Sara ran up to her and suddenly stopped. She got one of Vicky's evil smiles on her face.

"What – are – you – doing!" said Vicky as Sara backed her into a corner.

Then in the blink of an eye Sara hit Vicky across the face.

"You little!" screamed Vicky as she charged at Sara.

Knocking her down they flew across the hall hitting, kicking, punching, biting, pulling hair and other violent methods.

"You little brat," yelled Sara, getting on top of Vicky and punching her in the nose. Vicky then got on top of Sara and punched her in the nose. By the time a teacher got to them they were bleeding and hurt.

"Hey, hey you two stop it right now," said their principal, Mr. Carmatridge. "What are you doing! You two are going to be suspended for 4 weeks. Go! Go now and wait for me in my office while I call your parents."

While in the office the nurse came and helped their wounds. The nurse was a very nice person and everyone liked her. The whole school thought she was cool and funny.

"You know girls," she said as she was putting a bandage on Vicky's cheek and handing Sara an ice pack, "when I was a young girl I fought somebody."

"Who," asked Sara with a bloody lip.

"There was a very mean boy at school who always picked on me," she explained, "so one day I went to punch him. But when I got over there and swung at him he ducked. I ended up hitting this 4th grader in the eye. So I got suspended and I was in big, big trouble at home. So now you see you girls can't fight. What were you fighting about anyway?"

"Um…well you see Vicky has been picking on me and Chrissy Manson," Sara explained. "So one day on the weekend we decided to get her back. So we went to the mall with our dogs and had our puppies attack her. You know they were just puppies and they didn't bite her they just pinned her arms down. Then me and Chrissy took markers and drew all over her face."

"Oh, I see," said the nurse looking at Vicky's face.

Just then their mothers came in.

"Sara Kate Linn what on god's green earth have you done?" yelled Sara's mother.

"Vicky do you know I had to interrupt my boss in a conference to ask if I can leave," yelled Vicky's mom, "If I lose my job you are going to be grounded until high school!"

"Good morning, Mrs. Linn and Mrs. Miller," said Principal Carmatridge, "No this morning your two girls were fighting. Our school has a zero tolerance so they will have to be suspended for 4 weeks."

"What," yelled Sara.

"Sara, sit down," whispered her mother.

"Principal Carmatridge what my child is saying is that don't you think 4 weeks is a little harsh."

"O.k., he said, "how about 1 week suspension and 1 month of detention."

"Oh no," said Vicky, "I'm not going to detention or I'm not getting a suspension. Do you know how bad that will destroy my rep. Besides, Linn attacked me. I was only defending myself."

"Girls," said the Principal, "the punishment stands. Now go home. I will see you in a week."

***

"Hi," said Chrissy after she came home to school, "I told Lilly about the fight. She was really worried. Have you told Demon?"

"Yeah," said Sara, "He wanted a lot of details."

"Christina Mason," Chrissy's mom yelled, "You know Sara is grounded. We just came by to drop off her books. Let's go, hunny."

"O.K. mom," yelled Chrissy. "Bye! I'll call you later."

"O.k.," said Sara waving goodbye to Chrissy.

"Young lady you are grounded," said Chrissy's mom while walking home.

"Why?" yelled Chrissy in surprise.

"You know." said her mother, "You helped attack Vicky at the mall didn't you?"

"Well, I guess," said Chrissy.

"No, until Sara is out of suspension you will be grounded."

***

"Hi," said Sara later on the phone talking to Chrissy. "So you got in trouble too?"

"Yeah," said Chrissy, "for 1 week."

"Hey," said Sara, "do you want to meet at the tree house tonight at 9:00?"

"Sure," said Chrissy already excited, "and we can bring the dogs."

"O.K. So go to bed at nine and sneak out with Lilly to the tree house."

"Bye!" said Chrissy, "See you at nine."

***

At 9:00 Sara told her mom that she was going to bed. She grabbed Demon and headed out the window. She lived on the second floor so she used her sheets to make a rope.

As she headed to the tree house she saw Chrissy and Lilly there already.

"Hey," she said as she headed up the ladder.

By this time Chrissy and Sara had finally finished.

"So we can't see each other for a week," said Chrissy.

"And I can't see you at school because well...you know," said Sara.

"And even then you still have 1 month of detention. Now that's harsh," said Chrissy.

"Hey," said Demon, "Maybe every night around 9 we could meet here to talk."

"I think that is a good idea," said Lilly, "But we have to be home by 10:30."

"Deal," said Sara and Chrissy.

"And we could plot the most fun b-day party for Demon and Lilly," said Sara.

"Oh yes," Demon cried. "I'm going to be 4 months old."

"I'm so mature," said Lilly, "and very pretty."

***

On Friday they went and started getting ready for Saturday. They made a huge banner that said Happy b-day Demon and Lilly.

"I can't believe you're doing this just for the dogs," said Sara's mom as they set all of it up in the new tree house.

"Mom," asked Sara, "can we possibly get 2 big steak bones."

"And maybe 2 cupcakes for us," said Chrissy.

They covered the outside of the tree house with balloons and crepe paper.

"O.k. guys it's getting dark and we have to go eat dinner. Good thinking, I'm out of suspension Monday," said Sara.

"Bye," said Chrissy, "I think my mom is calling me. Come on Lilly."

The next day Sara and Chrissy woke up bright and early without waking Demon and Lilly up. Because they were going to add a little bit more to the party. They had a piñata that was shaped like a cat. It was filled with tiny bones and candy (for the girls not the dogs). Then they crept into their room and scooped up the puppies and headed for the tree house.

As the dogs finally woke up they almost fell over. Their Moms and Dads were also there.

"Mom! Dad!" yelled Demon. Demon's parents were named Tank and Claire. Lilly's parents were named Allie and Jamie.

"Happy B-day," yelled all of their parents. First they did presents. Chrissy got Demon a Frisbee. Sara got him a little tie. Tank got him a new leash. Claire got him a tennis ball. Chrissy got Lilly a bow. Sara got her a very cute collar. Allie got her a big turkey flavored bone. Jamie got her a big puppy blanket.

Then came the big bones. All the dogs got 1. And Sara and Chrissy got cupcakes.

"Piñata! Piñata!" shouted Lilly.

"Ok. OK calm down," said Chrissy pulling out a huge cat shaped piñata and a blue stick.

Demon, of course was up first. Sara picked him up and put the stick in his mouth. Then he swung hard and made a big dent in it. Then it was Lilly's turn.

"Oh she can't hit it hard," said Demon, "she's a girl."

As he said that Lilly stuck her tongue out at him. She took a huge swing at it and broke the head off. All of a sudden tons of candy and bones flowed out. Demon starred at her in disbelief.

"Ha!" she said as she walked past him and swung her tail in his face.

After that they convinced their parents to let them have a sleep over in the tree house. They stayed up all night. Just as they were going to bed Sara heard a noise coming from Chrissy's house.

"What was that?" asked Sara.

"What?" said Lilly very sleepy.

"Oh my god," said Chrissy all of a sudden bolting out of her sleeping bag, "I think there is someone trying to break into my house."

They quietly climbed out of the tree house and into the garage. They got 2 bats.

"Hey wait for us," said Demon while both he and Lilly were trying to catch up.

"Oh no," said Sara," this is way too dangerous for a couple of puppies. You two go back to the tree house now."

"But…" started Lilly.

"We said go," said Chrissy about to go in the door.

As they walked in it seemed that nothing was wrong. But as they turned the corner they saw that, where the dogs usually slept, Lilly's parents were gone! Both Sara's and Chrissy's parents had gone out today so they were not home.

All of a sudden Sara bolted out the door to her house. When Chrissy arrived she was bent over the empty dog bed crying.

"I know, I know," said Chrissy starting to cry herself.

Just then they heard a small creek. The door opened slowly and in came Demon and Lilly.

"Where are my Mommy and Daddy," asked Demon looking around and not seeing his parents anywhere.

"I don't know," said Sara, and Demon suddenly burst into tears and into Sara's arms as she held him and cried.

"It's O.K.," said Lilly, "you can share mine. I'm sure they won't mind."

"Ummm, Lilly," said Chrissy very slowly, "We went to our house and your mom and dad are not there either."

"So...so...so..." said Lilly as the tears filled up her tiny dark brown eyes, "I'm not going to see them anymore!"

She ran over to Chrissy and threw herself into Chrissy's arms and started sobbing.

"Don't worry," said Sara starting to pull herself together, "there has to be a clue around here somewhere. You guys are dogs so...you know start sniffing."

"Yeah," said Demon growing more confident about this, "I bet if we sniff out a clue we can catch them with our parents!"

"O.K.," said Chrissy, "split up."

As they searched the house they could not find anything for about an hour. Going around the room a 3rd time Lilly started to smell something odd.

"Hey," she called out to Demon, "get over here and smell this."

"Yeah," said Demon after he smelled it, "this is not your normal smell."

"You guys hurry up and come here," said Sara bent over a pile of knocked over magazines.

"What?" said Chrissy.

"Look, it's a flier. What does it say," said Lilly jumping up and down trying to see it.

"It says, 'stop the experimenting NOW,'" said Sara.

"What does that mean?" asked Demon.

"I know," said Chrissy all of a sudden, "They took your parents to experiment on. They probably ripped this off their building and dropped it here."

"Look what I found," said Lilly as she was sniffing at the front door.

"It's a pamphlet," said Sara picking up what was wedged under the mat.

"A pamphlet of what," asked Chrissy.

"Wait! Wait! Hold on," barked Demon, "What on dog's green earth is a hamphlet?"

"No...no...not a hamphlet a pamphlet," said Sara showing him the piece of paper.

"Yeah," said Lilly, "even for a girl I knew that." As soon as she walked away Demon stuck out his tongue and crossed his eyes.

"Oh," said Chrissy picking him up, "you are such a puppy."

"So what is the pamphlet about," said Lilly.

"It said 'Come down to California...we have the biggest factories in the whole U.S.' and at the very bottom in small print it listed some of their factories. And the very last one said 'Testing various products at the Experimental warehouse. Address: 24863 Maple Dr.' So what this is basically saying is that we have to go to California," said Sara with a sound of sadness in her voice.

Demon, Lilly and Chrissy looked at her and nodded.

"But...how," she asked curiously.

"Well first we have to leave a note for our parents," said Sara eagerly.

"Wait, should they come with us," asked Chrissy.

"Are you kidding," said Demon surprised that she even thought of that.

"Yeah," said Lilly, "you want to tell them you and your puppies, whom you can talk to, are going to California to chase down my parents and find their kidnappers."

"Yeah," said Sara, "and besides they would say it's too dangerous and that the dogs probably ran away."

"You're right," said Chrissy thinking about what her parents would say if they told them.

"But there is one problem," said Sara.

"What?" asked Demon.

"Money," said Chrissy reading Sara's mind.

"Wait," said Sara, "I know this is like stealing but my mom left her purse here because she said my dad was going to pay."

"Well," said Lilly, "I'm sure if you explain it to her that it is an emergency she will not be mad."

Another problem arose in Demon's mind. "They aren't just going to let kids and dogs on a plane to California," he said.

"Well get a costume," said Chrissy.

So they went up to Sara's mom's closet to find something that would make them look like her.

"Who am I supposed to be?" said Chrissy.

"You have to be the bottom of me," said Sara picking up a dress.

"Oh no I'm not going to have you on my shoulders all through the flight."

"Well," said Sara starting to protest, "what do you suppose we do?"

"Maybe she can be a friend accompanying you on your trip," said Lilly.

"There are 3 problems with that," said Sara, "#1 we would have to spend a lot of money on 2 tickets. #2 we are too short to pass as adults. And #3 she wouldn't have an I.D."

"Well," said Chrissy, "I've got 3 answers to that. #1 my mom left her purse at home also so I can pay for 1 ticket. #2 there can be short adults. #3 my mom has her I.D. in her purse."

"O.k., fine," said Sara.

"Not to rain on your parade or anything," said Lilly, "but you two don't look like your parents."

"I know," said Demon, "just put one of your pictures over it but you have to be dressed adultly."

"Yeah," agreed the girls.

So they dressed in their most adult looking cloths ever. Chrissy even put on her reading glasses. With all of this stuff they really looked like adults. So then Sara took a picture of Chrissy and vise-versa. Chrissy was a real computer freak. And so she took the digital camera and hooked it up to her computer. Then she minimized them so she could fit them into the I.D. photo space. Then she printed them out. Sara cut them out and taped them to the I.D., being careful not to show any tape. When they were finished they looked very proud.

"We have to pack," said Sara.

So each of them went and got a suitcase. Even Lilly and Demon got one.

"Um," said Chrissy, trying not to laugh, "you guys are so cute in thinking you need suitcases."

"Well," said Demon looking at all of his stuff, "we need to bring it all don't' we?"

"No," said Sara, coming into the room carrying her suitcase full of cloths and stuff, "only the things you need."

Chrissy ran and got their book bags. "You guys can fill this up with your toys and your favorite little treats for the plane ride there."

Once they were packed all of them stopped at the door and looked out.

"Guys do you know what I'm thinking," said Sara.

"Yeah," said Chrissy, "how are we going to get there."

"Well," said Demon, "you can't expect us to walk the whole way there."

"Of course not," said Chrissy, trying to think of a way to get themselves to the airport.

"Well," said Sara, "the airport is only a few blocks away from the Taco Bell so if we get my aunt to drive us there we can just walk to the airport."

"Are you sure this will work," said Lilly.

"Yes, I'm sure," said Sara with a grunt. She ran to the phone and called her aunt.

"Hello…Aunt Barbra. Yeah it's me. I was wondering if you could drive my friend and me to Taco Bell. You could just leave us there and my mom will pick us up after were done. You can. Thanks a lot. Bye bye."

She hung up the phone with a smile.

"So we're really gonna do this," said Chrissy staring at her best friend.

"Yeah," said Sara. "Think about it a couple of weeks ago we were just 2 girls with puppies. Now we're flying off to go save our puppies parents."

"Wow," said Lilly, "You know…" she paused and told them to come closer and away from Demon. "I…think I might have a crush on Demon."

The girls looked at each other with surprise.

"Really?" asked Sara.

"Yeah," she said a little shy, "I would probably be turning red right now if it weren't for my fur."

The girls giggled at this.

"What'd I say?" asked Lilly innocently.

A Planet Called Earth

Captain,

I arrived here on Earth three days ago. I must say three days was enough. I chose the United States of America for the place to conduct my studies. I have seen that this land mass was at the heart of civilization, so it only makes sense to spend my time here. Through my studies, I have seen that this planet was once lush, green, and full of a huge variety of species. But it seems that, over centuries, one species began to dominate. They call themselves humans. And they have turned this green and blue orb into a fast-paced, terrifying concrete world.

I say this because they multiply so fast that other species are pushed off into the boundaries and sometimes die off, never to live again. I have studied their cultures, politics, and literature. I have learned their ways and have guised myself under the name Adam. He was one of the first humans believed to exist and I find it very dignified. I will continue my research and report further. This planet called Earth looks promising, but only the beings on it are able to make it succeed.

~ Optimistically, Adam

Captain,

The horrors I have witnessed. Man is not a kind creature. Never in my existence have I seen one species be so divided. I see them as humans, one no different than the other. But they can't seem to do the same. They are absorbed in themselves and feel the need to put labels on each other. Black, White, Jewish, Muslim. How can they possibly survive in the future if this is what goes on? Are they so ignorant that they divide themselves when this is the time to unite? Captain, my hope dwindles more each hour.

~ Desperately, Adam

***

Captain,

Starvation occurs while others relish in luxury. Men kill men, themselves not understanding why they are doing it. Give a man a gun and he will shoot; it seems like the main concept of "war." By nature I have seen this happen, but not to this great a scale. For principle, People are willing to bomb entire masses of innocent people. It is sickening. I believe that this is what tears this planet apart.

Today I walked through the streets of New York City. The machines of the modern ages and the huge buildings that loomed in the sky were at every turn I took. I think that the outstanding number of begging, suffering people can only be matched by the indifferent people. The people who see these faces and choose to ignore them, as if they are not human. Does one lose one's identity when in the need of help? Are they all of a sudden not human and less important? As an outsider I see them for what they are: selfish. Utterly selfish and centered. They do not see their own insignificance, and this may be their downfall.

I am homesick now, so very homesick. I look to the sky out of my apartment window, but the stars aren't there. I can't see them from here.

I cried tonight over this diminishing planet. Such a strange feeling it was.

~ Sorrowfully, Adam

***

Captain,

A moment occurred which made me look up at the sky to the star they call "Sun."

I trudged into the park today, not hoping for anything. Crossing the streets I heard words yelled at people, their only purpose to hurt. Why is this? I am tired of trying to understand.

I sat on a bench, my head in my hands. When you sent me on this study, Captain, I assumed I would encounter something adventurous. Something exciting. Never did I realize that the research I gathered at this planet would change me. I pity them. If only they could see.

That was when I looked up and saw her walking towards me. The dimpled face and blonde pigtails all looked up at me, smiling. Ice cream was smeared on her cheeks and chin and the knees of her pink overalls were stained green.

"Hi," she said trustingly. She sat beside me and looked over, feet swinging inches off the ground. She held one sticky hand out to me. I grinned and shook it.

"Amber," her mother came up beside her. "Leave that man alone. It's time to go." She looked up at me and mouthed 'sorry.' I laughed.

Amber sighed and got up. On a moment's thought she reached into her pocket and pulled out a crumpled piece of paper. She took my hand and placed the ball in it. "You look like you need it," she explained seriously. Her mother smiled gently and took the young girls hand.

As she walked off, Amber looked over her shoulder and waved. My hand lifted in response.

Captain, I am still thinking about that little girl. I have decided that she is all the hope that this planet has. Taking care of Earth will be put into her hands one day. Into those sticky little hands. I only hope that she can learn from the mistakes of her elders and do right. Because if the Earth makes it into the future years, it will be because of little Amber and the humans of that generation.

I look into my hands and pick the paper up. It is a tiny paper heart, scribbled in lightly with red crayon. I smiled into the sky and felt the breeze brush my face. That is one of the things I will miss about Earth, the magnificence of the wind.

I now see that all this planet needs is love. And, here, love is all around, you just have to know what to look for.

~ Simply, Adam

Forgetting[14]

Nora blinked.

She had woken up in the middle of the night again, confused and unsure. She relaxed into her bed, her head easing into the pillow. She breathed in deeply and slow. She was home.

She was dreaming again. Usually when she slept it was nothing, just darkness. But now they were back. Vivid dreams of another life, another Nora.

She was so tired of these dreams, exhausted. When she dreamt she always felt scared, and she could never remember why. She was just scared; scared of the future and of forgetting. Forgetting...something. It was just beyond her memory.

But that was over now. Nora knew that, during the day, she would be fine. It was the night that she was worried about.

She walked out of her room in a daze. Nora felt...good today. Better then she had in a long time. Her long dark hair was finally co-operating itself and she felt healthy enough for a run around the block.

Nora neared the door when a hand stopped her in her tracks.

"Nora dear, what are you doing up this early?"

"Oh...Mary." Nora turned slowly. "I was having nightmares again and well...I thought that I might go for a run today. I have been feeling so good and –"

---

[14] Editor's note: "Forgetting" is one of Allie's stories from Kaleidoscope, her high school writing club's magazine.

"Now you know that's silly." Mary cut her off, "Go on and get ready for breakfast. You need your strength honey."

As Nora stalked off she looked over her situation. Living in a home for young girls wasn't ideal for her life. All the rules and expectations were stifling. She needed to get out, escape and live her life. Before it was too late.

"Oh Mary!" She called down, "After breakfast can I go meet Jim in the park?"

"I suppose." Mary hesitated. "But you have to be careful this time." She added, "We don't need you to get any worse."

Nora sighed. It was just like Mary to always worry about her health. There were many other girls here that were worse than her. Thinking about it made her sad. Sometimes this place could get very depressing

***

It was a cool autumn day. The wind blew her hair around her face as she took a seat next to Jim on the bench.

He smiled kindly toward her, his eyes bright. "Hello Nora. How is it today?"

She frowned, "How is what? Why is everyone acting so strange to me lately?" She glanced away irritated. "I can't wait to get out. I'll leave this place so far behind me."

"Oh...yes I see," he whispered. He looked down at his feet. "Has it gotten that bad?"

Nora looked away. Sometimes Jim and the others got into a mood like this. She just nodded and pretended to listen.

Jim took her hand in his. She smiled shyly. He was always so nice to her. She couldn't tolerate this place without seeing him, almost daily.

"I just wanted to tell you that I'm leaving soon. My family has finally come to pick me up. I'll be going home."

It was so sudden that it took Nora a minute to fully register what he was saying. She stared at him, holding back the tears. "I'm happy for you...really I am." She dropped her smile and brushed her hair out of her eyes. "Maybe someday it will happen for me."

"Don't give up hope Nora. Just...don't give up," he pleaded. He stood up and brushed himself. "Now I've got to be going."

He looked her deep in the eyes and Nora blushed, despite herself. "Please...just promise you won't forget me. Please stay well Nora."

"Of course I will," she said quietly. She didn't really know what Jim was talking about but she didn't want to ruin this moment. Not now.

"Remember to write me!" she yelled after him. He looked back over his shoulder and blew her a kiss.

Nora sat there for a while. Things were changing around her and she didn't like it. Everything was moving ahead, but it always seemed liked she was the one that stayed the same, the one left watching as they walked off...into the future.

She cradled her head in her hands. It was going to be a long day.

***

"Nora you have some people here to visit you."

As Nora walked through the door she saw her mother and sisters standing by the dinner tables. Her mood brightened instantly and she ran over and hugged them tightly. After Jim left, she needed something to comfort her.

"Mom, I'm so glad you came to visit. Things haven't been going so good."

Her mother shared a worried look between her sisters. Nora had seen this look before. She had no idea what was wrong with everyone today.

"Honey, I'm so happy to see you too. Have you been doing well?"

Her mother's eyes were staring off in the distance, not looking at Nora's face.

"Um...yeah sure. Everything's fine."

"That's good," she sighed. "I'm going to talk with Mary now. You go on and visit with your...," she paused, "your sisters."

Had she been crying today? Nora shrugged. Maybe that's what the outside world did to people now, changed them. Maybe that was the reason why they wouldn't take her home yet.

"Jill...and Lisa!" Nora turned her attention to her sisters. "How have you guys been? How is the family?"

Nora looked on eagerly. Both girls looked strikingly like her. Tall and thin, with wild black hair.

Jill nervously fidgeted in her seat. "We've been fine and everyone is great at home." She looked Nora's eyes. "We all miss you."

Lisa looked at her hands, not saying a word. At 7 Lisa didn't speak much, at least not to Nora.

She sighed and smiled sadly at them. The attitude of her family would never change. Always pitying her and Nora could never figure out why. But she wasn't one for confrontation with her family.

She looked over her shoulder to her mother. She was talking with Mary feverishly. Tears streamed down her face as she turned to Nora.

Nora scowled at the table. It was so frustrating not being able to know important things about your own family. She felt...helpless.

Her mother walked over and hugged her tight. "Get better please. And stay safe." She grabbed Lisa and Jill and started to walk to the door.

Nora stood, "But...you're leaving? So soon?" She walked towards the door, her voice rising slightly. "When will you be back? When can I go home?" She was close to tears having to watch them walk away...again. Why was everyone in her life always walking away?

"Get some sleep!" her mother yelled as she walked out the door. "I love you!"

Nora stared silently at the door. Anger welled up inside her. How could she think things would actually change? Nothing ever did. Nothing ever would.

She ran up to her room and closed the door. Then, and only then, would she let herself cry. Breakdown and let all the emotions free.

***

Nora got into bed that night feeling defeated. Life would never get better and on top of all of it were the dreams. Remembering them made her shudder.

She was always in a dark room with another person. The light would come on, low and flickering. An older version of her self would be standing there in the shallow light. The woman stared back defiantly, worn out with a crazy look about her.

"Where? Where? *Where?*"

She would search the darkness confused. All the time repeating that word, over and over.

Then suddenly she would go still and walk towards Nora. She could remember the smell of her breath and her yellowed teeth. Nora would look up hesitantly into those two bloodshot muddied eyes. Old Nora would lean in close and whisper raggedly.

"I. Can't. Remember."

Then Nora would wake up and return to her everyday normal life, all the while trying to forget the awful dream that never stopped.

Nora shut off the lamp and breathed deep. She braced herself and closed her eyes, slowly drifting off to sleep.

***

Mary looked into Nora's room with sadness. A young nurse stepped up beside her.

"What's wrong?" She asked looking into Mary's face.

"It's Nora. She's getting worse. Her delusions are so advanced that we are afraid to let her out of the nursing home."

The nurse peered into the small room. "She looks so frail? What's wrong with her?"

Mary wiped at her eyes. "At 65 she has a large tumor in her brain. Inoperable, it's slowly killing her. We try to keep in the present... in this life. But her fantasies are so great that we're losing her more each day."

"How long has she been like this?"

Mary closed her eyes. "I think it began to worsen when her friend Jim Morgan passed. They used to talk every day. That was 5 months ago." She looked back into the room with such love.

"Just today I talked with her daughter. It was so sad. She brought her two young granddaughters in to visit. It broke my heart to tell her that it won't be long now."

The nurse hugged Mary sympathetically. "For all my years here," Mary sighed, "Nora has touched my life the most. I'll never forget her."

They both stood in silence. The light from the hallway shone in the darkened room illuminating Nora's face. Mary slowly closed the door, as to not disturb her.

The beam of light narrowed to a sliver....then was gone.

Nora woke up stiff from sleep. She shook away her dream and looked outside at the brightening sky.

Today was going to be different. She would talk with Jim and hopefully see her family. Maybe they would take her home soon. Yes, today would be different.

Ocean's Spray

Long ago a Queen in a faraway land was expecting her first child. To an oracle she went, but the old woman told her terrible news. "Your son will bring misfortune to your family and eventually cause your downfall and the destruction of the Earth itself."

The terrified Queen pleaded with the old woman to tell her a way to stop her son. The woman took pity on the Queen.

"A sure way to stop this disaster is to swim to the ocean's bottom and chain your newborn son to the ground."

"But," the old woman warned pointing a crooked finger in the Queen's face, "you must remember to give a sacrifice to the Sea Walker, Camina. Only when this is done will she let you pass into her waters and perform your task." The Queen nodded and set out to perform such a task.

Two months later the Queen got an unexpected visitor to the palace. The old woman was dragged away by the guards and the Queen did nothing to stop this, fearing her husband would find out about the fate of their son.

While being dragged away the old woman shouted her message, "The time has come my dear! Go! Go and do as I said! Hurry before you doom us all!" The Queen heard this and soon prepared to leave the palace.

Later that night the young Queen snuck out of the palace and walked to the shore of the sea. Pulling out a basket, the Queen laid fruits and meat at the water's edge. The sacrifice having been made, the Queen took a deep breath and stepped into the water. To her shock the old woman stood before her, water swirling all around her. To the Queen's further astonishment, the old woman suddenly began to transform. When the waters finally settled the beautiful goddess Camina stood before the young queen, brilliant and powerful. "You have disrespected me by first coming for help and then not allowing me into your home, when I have done a great service to you." The queen shook with fright but did not turn to leave, she had come here to do something and she would not leave until it was accomplished. "But," the Ship Destroyer continued, "since you have brought me a sacrifice I will let you do what you came to do. However, as punishment to your ungratefulness to a helpless person, you will be sentenced to spend your life caring for the son you banish to the sea."

Before the Queen could object, a swarm of fish engulfed her. When the fish scattered the queen had in her arms a beautiful blond baby boy. "Now don't be fooled," Camina warned, "this is the monster that will bring an end to your species forever." So with sadness the Queen put her baby on the floor and looked away as the creatures of the sea began to bind him with chains, thus ensuring he stayed forever imprisoned.

To this day the Queen and her son, named Tyvan the merciless, are still at the bottom of the sea, for all eternity. Tyvan's strength was so great that he could take the waters of the ocean and hurl them at masses of land, creating giant sprays of water for the people above to wonder about. But as always, the Queen would come to her son's aid and calm him, therefore calming the oceans.

It is said that at times the Queen was allowed to visit the land above and the people above. At these times Tyvan grew especially infuriated and pushed the ocean towards the land, trying to get his mother back to him. When she did return, always by Carnina's order, the waters retreated, also known as low tide.

An Influential Person in my Life[15]

I come from a very family orientated family. For my entire life, I have always known my family would be there for me. It is a nice, safe feeling that a person should have when growing up. If I ever need anything, whether it would be a cup of sugar or a place to sleep, I would only have to walk down the street to the nearest Aunt or Uncle. However, I would say that the most influential person in my life would have been my grandmother.

My grandma on my mother's side lived just five minutes away. I would visit her many times during the week just to check in. Sitting with her and talking are still some of the best memories that I can recall. Then, when I was in eighth grade, her health started to deteriorate. She was diagnosed with multiple types of cancer and we all knew that her time was short. It was very hard on me seeing the person that I looked up to reduced to a frail looking woman sitting in a hospital bed.

It was a hard time for me, but when she passed I tried not to mourn her, but instead remember her. She was there for me when I grew up and she helped me through my parents' divorce. I learned a lot from her and I will always be thankful that she was in my life for even a short period of time. I believe, however, that the biggest thing that she was able to teach me, just by being herself and following her own values, was that family is everything. She made me believe that I still had family all around, even when I experienced my own breaking apart. She let me know that I should not be afraid to look for help from those closest to me. I feel that this can help me in the future and lead me to follow my heart.

---

[15] Editor's note: In memory of Antoinette Collofello.

Alternate Ending to Speaking of Courage

Paul didn't want to go home that night. Just like last night, and the night before that. He walked slowly down the street after having parked his car in the garage. The neighbor's house was alight. Happy voices poured from it, resonating through the neighborhood.

Paul walked around to the back door of the house. His father sat lazily with the neighbors, talking loudly and drunkenly about nothing in particular. They sat there, watching the last of the fireworks die off in the night sky. That sporadic booming sound reminded Paul of something, something he didn't want to talk about.

Paul approached his father; words that were longing to be said lay in his mouth, solid and heavy. His dad looked up and saw Paul, standing awkwardly by the gate.

"I gotta go boys," he grumbled, struggling to move himself out of the lawn chair. "Thanks for the show. See ya tomorrow."

He stumbled over to Paul and Paul led him out the gate and back onto the streets. "How was your night boy?"

"Fine," Paul answered. The longing in his heart was so achingly painful that he had to speak up, just once, before this night was over.

"Dad, I just wanted to talk – "

"It's fourth of July," his father interrupted. "I wanted to thank you."

Their slow, lazy pace down the street had stopped. Paul's father turned to him. The moon was out, bright and full. From the meager light, Paul could see how old his father was. Not just his appearance, but also his spirit. His will to live.

The way his eyes used to sparkle with life – that was gone. You could see the shadows of death holding tight under his eyes. You could see the sad way his mouth fell when he wasn't holding it up. You could see the war all over his face. The gruesome, terrible things that he had experienced were written on the face of an average middle-aged man. There he was, his father, standing in front of Paul, drunk and desperately unhappy.

Well, at least that was what Paul saw. *Do* I *look like that?* Paul vaguely wondered.

"Thank you," his father repeated. The walls and barricades were up again, forcing Paul away. A moment before, however, Paul could swear he saw something in his father's eyes. In any sense, it was gone now, perhaps forever. Paul ran through all the words stored in his mind that he had been longing to say so badly earlier. He shrugged a little and started walking again.

"You're welcome," he said casually.

A Call of Heroism

The bolded paragraphs are actual conversations held between the operators and the people who called 911. All calls that are used were handled by the Emergency Medical Services. The callers' statements have been redacted to ensure the privacy of these individuals. All information was gathered from an article by the Washington Post.

This story was written to commemorate all the heroic people who contributed to the aid of thousands of people on September 11th. The operators at the New York City Fire Department worked days on end. With their help many people trapped in the buildings of the World Trade Center were able to be rescued. The information they provided and the aid they gave saved lives. You are the heroes of the modern day, and we thank you.[16]

CRO: That is so bad, you know. That's so sad, AC. You know --

OPERATOR: It is.

CRO: On the 83rd --

OPERATOR: I can't imagine.

CRO: Oh, God. You be trapped, something like that -- we've got the 83rd – on the second World Trade Center on the 83rd floor five people were trapped, went unconscious. I don't know what they're doing. And it's an awful thing, it's an awful, awful, awful thing to call somebody

---

[16] Allison included these notes – and her thanks – just before the story that follows.

and tell them you're going to die. That's an awful thing. I hope -- I hope they're all alive because they sound like they went -- they passed out because they were breathing hard, like snoring, like they're unconscious.

OPERATOR: Right.

CRO: That's an awful, awful thing. And nobody probably really knows about them, because it's the second World Trade Center and all the calls were being -- I mean, they know now, but, you know, at first.

OPERATOR: Right.

Just another day. Now when I look back, I wish it was true. I used to say that my life was boring and that I wanted excitement. But nothing like what happened, oh God, nothing like that. I woke up that morning like usual. I really had no idea that this day would change my life.

I like the feeling of helping people. I really do. That's why I trained so many hours to be with the crisis response operations. I feel that I'm level headed and can be cool during a disaster. There is nothing like a catastrophe that puts everything in perspective. I was young back then. I wasn't prepared. No one was. That's the scariest part.

OPERATOR: I changed -- I changed the code.

CRO: It's sad. It's sad. It's sad. I'm excited I'm afraid. That is. That's right. Okay. Thank you. I just wanted to make sure, AC, because--

OPERATOR: All right. No problem.

CRO: No, no, listen. We have to communicate. It would be easier, they may need additional units. And if you don't tell the supervisor -- now

what I do and what you do is you document you spoke to a lieutenant. So if God forbid they need additional units and they were not sent for, you covered yourself right now.

I heard the first explosion. Loud and clear. I can recall the feeling of total disaster. I mildly remember thinking that Armageddon had come. Our time was over. I guess for many it seemed like Armageddon: a sort of Hell on Earth.

The phones went crazy after that. Sophie looked over, eyes wide and fearful. I mentally sent her strength. I have been in situations where terrible things have happened. After a while you get a feeling if something major has happened. Like another sense. And today I knew this was going to be a big one.

CALLER: [redacted]

CRO: We can't tell you what to do because God forbid -- I mean, I'm sorry, we're not in your situation.

An accident? A plane crash? I really had no details. I just kept my head down and dealt with each call at a time.

But there were so many. Determination turned to desperation. No way could they get there in time. No way could so many people be saved. I knew that deep down, but our job is to provide hope to people in desperate situations. I repeated the advice that I was given.

Keep low to the ground. Wet towels over your heads. Don't break the window; it may let more smoke in.

CRO: Stay calm. I agree with you that you need air, but I can't tell you to break a window. Now, I can tell you if you break the window you might let more smoke or debris in.

CALLER: [redacted]

CRO: Okay. And then if you break the window, will you break your foundation more. You know what I'm saying? So we can't, so I can't say --

"Please sir, calm down. You need to hear what I have to say."

"Sir everyone is there, trying to help. It's just a matter of getting up to your floor."

"Ma'am. Ma'am, are you there? Hello?"

Too many lines going dead. What was happening up there? How many lives were going to end today? I had a feeling that the number was going to be great.

"Jimmy," Sophie called desperately in my direction, "Jimmy the computers, they aren't working. I...I can't get the information in. Oh Lord...JIMMY."

The last word ended in a screech. She was still taking calls, the tears muffled her speech.

"Calm down, calm down, calm down." My prayer. It was more to keep myself coherent then to aid the others. I needed time. I needed more information. There were too many calls. How was I supposed to help these people? How??

CRO: On moment sir. Everything – our computers are messing up.

I wiped my eyes. This was no time to get emotional. We are the people that need to be calm. We are the people that handle the emergencies.

CRO: Another plane now?

OPERATOR: Another plane. This is a whole new thing now.

CRO: Okay. All right. What is going on?

OPERATOR: They're saying it might be a terrorist attack.

CRO: Oh. Okay.

OPERATOR: It would have to be because what are the odds of two planes crashing into the same building; okay? That is just –

CRO: Ironic. Let me see. Now our system is down.

OPERATOR: Your system is down?

CRO: Oh, my goodness.

Terrorists. That's a good name. There was plenty of terror that day. A second plane could be no accident. At least this gave me information to relay on. So many scared and confused people. They needed to know what had just happened to them.

This wasn't an accident. It just kept repeating in my mind. It wasn't an accident. In my lifetime I have never seen such horror be done to another human.

This was beyond horror. This was fear. An agonizingly true fear. No more monsters under the bed to be afraid of, no more childish worries. This fear was true. This fear was death. This fear became a reality that very moment.

CRO: Okay, listen. Just calm down. If you guys panic –

CALLER: [redacted]

CRO: Okay, listen, listen, listen to me, listen to me; okay? Listen, don't – try not to panic. You can save your air supply by doing that; okay?

CALLER: [redacted]

CRO: All right. Try not to panic. I understand what – do you have a towel, sir? Do you have a towel? Do you have a towel?

CALLER: [redacted]

CRO: Okay. Calm yourself down.

What could I do? Give them advice they already know, say to them that the firefighters are on their way? That was just a false hope, an empty statement. Each time this fell from my lips to be received by the grasping ear of the victims, I uttered a prayer. A desperate plea to God that these people would be saved. These screaming, helpless people would be alright. That it wouldn't be their time to go. Not now God, not now.

CRO: Okay, listen. Listen to me. Listen to me. Listen, the fire – if the fire is underneath you, somebody needs to look and see if the fire is on top of you also.

CALLER: [redacted]

CRO: Find another staircase and see if you can make it upstairs.

CALLER: [redacted]

CRO: Okay.

OPERATOR: He hung up.

CRO: Oh, God. All right.

"Don't worry, I will stay on the line with you. Help is coming.

I wanted to be there with them. Comforting and helpful. But every time I heard the phone die, I shuddered. I can't give up. I can't give up for their sake.

During this time, I remember thinking of the brave firefighters. Come on boys, come on. You can do this.

CRO: What's the matter? Are you having difficulty breathing. Are you on the 100th floor? What room number? AC, do you have a room number to this?

OPERATOR: No, it's a cell caller. I have no room, nothing.

CRO: Talk to me, ma'am. Take control of yourself. Ma'am, how old are you. Ma'am, hello? AC?

OPERATOR: Yes.

CRO: Oh, God.

OPERATOR: What I got from her is 100th floor, World Trade Center.

CRO: She was able to speak?

OPERATOR: Just barely. That's all I got. I don't know what company, what room. No telephone number, nothing.

The helplessness was overwhelming. I wanted to cry. I wanted to scream.

But, no. This was my duty. My responsibility to these frightened people. I had to keep composure. At least for a little while.

The calls were mad. Something happens to people in a disaster; something strange. There are those who panic and those who take charge. The calm, levelheaded people are those that we call heroes.

Those are the people who saved lives on September 11th.

CRO (to lieutenant): Lieutenant, I've got a guy on the 106th floor and he wants to know how to deal with a hundred people. He wants some directions. I don't know.

The day ended, amazingly. I was relieved of my position sometime during the night. My part in this nightmare was over.

OPERATOR: This will be a new job, because this is a rescue.

CRO: The whole thing is a rescue.

I have always wondered during the many sleepless nights that followed…did I help that day? Did I save someone's life? I can't expect anything to come. No pride, no honor, no relief. I'm still just amazed. Amazed at what I experienced that day. Humanity is frail and breakable. We live our lives on a very precarious edge.

That day I felt like I jumped off the edge. I saw death in every doorway I passed. It was on the faces of my friends and neighbors. It was looking at me from every newspaper and television channel. It was deeply embedded into my heart.

You would have never thought that you would experience this sort of thing. It doesn't happen.

However, on that day, the hearts and eyes of every American were opened. And the memories of the ones we lost are forever with us.

"I've been scared before, but 9/11 showed me that fear comes in varying magnitudes. On that day, fear was a physical presence sitting in

the room with us as we watched the instantaneous obliteration of thousands of lives, just two street corners away. I pray that I never have to feel that scared again." – Chetan Acharya; eyewitness

City Violence

Maggie jumped.

Her hair flew out behind her and her scream died on the wind. But she wasn't too worried, this was life for her.

***

Maggie Fisher took her job seriously; I mean who wouldn't when you were a hired assassin. She glanced at the time. Almost nine, in a half an hour she would leave and come back late into the night, exhausted and emotionally worn. Those were the things that followed a job, and after every hit Maggie became more stone and less human, and so cold she found that she would never thaw. Better to just push the emotions down and deal with them at another time.

Her black hair was tied up in a tight bun; she always hated having it in her way when she was working. She had thought about cutting it but then she wouldn't have that one memory from the past, where she was young and not so hardened and her mother used to comb her long hair each day. Maggie looked exactly like her mother, except she was tan while her mother was sickly white, possibly foreshadowing what was to come. When the cancer had come it was the hardest thing to watch her hair fall out. After that Maggie was on her own, just the way she liked it. At twenty three her mother had probably expected her to be out of college and fulfilling her dreams. Well, her dreams had died with her mother so Maggie was not too upset with her current life; she just hoped that her mother was not disappointed.

She grabbed her coat and headed out into the cold nighttime air. Maggie loved the city and all that came with it. The smells, the people, and the complete familiarity of what Maggie does. The city has never been ashamed or disappointed in what she has done. It grimly accepts it as a part of life and moves on, never glancing back, always on the move. That is one reason Maggie chose this spot on the globe to live, because it fit her profession. And to Maggie, her profession was her life.

Daren had been very specific for the circumstances of how this latest job was going to go down. And she was not to fail on this one, not in any way. But really Maggie had barely listened to what Daren had said that day, she was too focused on his face. He had a handsome face and green eyes that could kill. And that was what he did to Maggie every time he met up with her to deliver her assignment. He killed her and didn't even know it. From her tentative start in this career Maggie always had Daren. He was her best friend and knew her more than anyone in her life had ever known. However just as Daren was amazingly brilliant, he was also blindly ignorant toward her and her feelings. But those were some of the feelings she pushed deep inside her, and one way that got rid of those feelings every time was doing her job.

She stepped onto the road and looked toward the park. This was the place they had agreed upon. Night and deserted, perfect meeting spot with an imperfect man. And this man was imperfect, deadly to a point. She paused under a street light to review her case.

Gerald Gizard, aka "Gizmo."

The scum had a big record. Twenty-two bank robberies all over the east coast, eighteen accounts of assault, and suspected accomplice in the murder of a 9 year old girl. How had the authorities not caught this man yet? Well, this might have been good because where the police failed, Maggie didn't.

She walked into the park as casually as she could, scanning the trees for any signs of witnesses, you couldn't be too careful. She sat on a swing and gently rocked back and forth, the creaking alerting anyone near about her whereabouts. He emerged from the shadows just as she knew he would, still she froze with what could have been called terror. But Maggie never felt terror so you would have to call it something else.

Maggie and Daren had arranged for this meeting to go a certain way. Maggie flashed the package and he walked up to her quickly, constantly looking over his shoulders. The stolen jewelry was real, and if Maggie had any sort of conscience she would feel guilty, but sometimes you need to break the law to draw out a criminal in hiding.

Maggie stood as he came near, holding the bag out in front of her.

"Show it to me first," the squeaky voice certainly did not fit the large man who stood in front of her.

His hood fell back as she poured the contents into her hand, and she looked upon the face of a true criminal. His hooked nose did take away from the sunken red eyes that stared at her hungrily. The red greasy hair was shaven close to his skull and the red scars shone bright against the pale skin of his face. This was perhaps the product of his jail time two years before. Or maybe, she thought, someone this devoid of good character was made to look on the outside as he did on the inside. He stumbled over and Maggie deduced that he was under the influence of something, which made her job easier.

"The deal is for you to take it to your connection and you will receive twenty percent when you deliver." Maggie smiled and added, "And of course we will supply a large quantity for your 'needs.'"

He shook his head in understanding and grabbed the bag from her, his hands shaky.

"No problem," he looked her up and down, "and maybe I might pay a little extra for time with you."

He reached for her arm by her side. Maggie saw her opportunity, when he was fully extended, intending to grab her, she would bring him down and finish her job. Moving slightly she caught an unexpected flash in the corner of her eye.

The boy took both of them down in one leap, and she bounced on the hard pavement hitting her head. When she glanced up the boy, about sixteen, was beating helpless Gizmo, his masked face showing no emotion. She sat still cradling her pounding and bleeding head until he noticed her and advanced toward her also.

His anger seemed to swell as he walked over to her and pulled her up, fully ready to punish Maggie as he had this evil man. Maggie bounced up lightly and kicked the youth to the ground, pulling out her revolver and pressing it to his skull. His arms were pinned under her knees and his feet flailed uselessly around behind her. Smiling she pulled off his cheap ski mask.

"Get off me," the boy harshly whispered, tears of hatred streaming down his face. "He deserved to die for what he did to my sister. She was all I had and he took her from me. All people like that should die."

"Well then we are agreed," she sighed and stood over him, this man was doomed from the moment he committed these crimes. When I was notified that my services were needed I was glad to help deliver the punishment. But you...you are young and hatred has blinded you. Never should a child be forced to deliver punishment to the unjust."

Gizmo moaned and rolled over, facing them. His face was beaten fairly well, but she assumed he would survive.

"You have to leave now. He is not worth whatever you think he might be, for if you do commit this act, it will stay with you forever. Now...," she gestured to him.

"Jason," he responded to her unasked question.

"Ok. Jason ask yourself, are you ready to take another human being's life? Are you ready to bear the burden and horror this will bring you? For once you kill, you may never take it back. Once you destroy something of your own free will, you are forever broken. Take it from someone who has been doing it for years."

She pushed a stray hair behind her ear and turned away from his emotionless face. He paused and looked back to Gizmo. By now he had fallen into unconsciousness and was breathing shallowly. He hurried after her fading form.

"Wait!" he called after her, searching the darkness for a face to the voice. She turned in the darkness. "What do I do now?"

"Live Jason. Use your anger not to hurt, but to help. Show that you are better than most people in this city." Her voice was becoming softer and softer as she left. After sometime she called back again. "The police are on their way. They won't suspect anything from a beaten man, but they will be looking around awhile. Go home and lay low for a while."

"Thank you," he called not knowing whether she had heard him or not. He would never know if she remembered him but for the rest of his life he would know who had saved him. And he would be forever thankful.

***

Maggie breathed the air deeply into her lungs. The great outdoors never got any better than this. She looked over the edge and saw Daren emerge from the water with a silly grin on his face. Cliff diving. This is what she chose to do for her vacation time. And even though it might have been dangerous it made her feel alive, which was a curious thing considering what she does for a living.

The city was a beautiful place but sometimes it was nice to be where nature wasn't so indifferent. The lake below her and waterfall to her right reminded her that even though parts of this world didn't care, there were also some parts of it that did. They remembered the past and hoped for the future.

Maybe this little "vacation" would become permanent. Maybe the city just wasn't for her. That life seemed so far away now, as if the two worlds were centuries apart, one untouched and the other ravaged. Thinking like this was what made Maggie need a vacation. And she took the opportunity, dragging along Daren to experience this joy with her.

The sun was bright and Maggie didn't feel as cold anymore. She didn't quite feel like stone. As if, the longer she stayed like this, in this place, thinking like this, the feelings would slowly rise out of that place she pushed them, and she might feel whole again. It might take a while, most likely until the day she died, but if she worked hard, she might one day finally heal her soul.

"Mags. If you don't jump then I'm taking the keys and leaving you up there." Daren was probably joking, hopefully, but Maggie was never one to be afraid. She lingered with her toes just over the edge, dangling, living in the fear that she had not felt since her mother had died. She could see her mother's calm face right now, and she looked happy.

She smiled at the memory, stole one last look at the sky, and jumped.

In Fate's Eye

Who knows what the future holds for us? One of human kind's greatest mysteries is knowing the future before it has yet to happen. But nothing is ever set in stone and one's destiny can change within a blink of an eye. My name is Samantha Nelson. Age 23. Height – 6 feet, and that is if I am wearing heels. Weight – well that's for me to know. Just an average New Yorker going about business in her very average life. My glamorous job as a post office worker has put me through college and is going pretty well. Just an average girl living with a not-so average secret.

I was in eighth grade when I had my first vision, if you could even call it a vision. Sitting in the park reading it was a beautiful afternoon and for once everything felt peaceful.

Now I admit I have a weird habit of people watching. It is not as creepy as some believe it to be. Observing the people around me I can see how life affects all of us differently. There is that one person always rushing to be somewhere important, nearly knocking everyone out of the way. There are the attention grabbers and the ones that just want to crawl in a hole and disappear.

And then there are the special ones. The ones like me who take in their surroundings and really appreciate everything in their lives. I mean isn't it a great gift, being able to live on this wonderful planet and just being alive. Most people take it for granted, and I admit I used to be one of those people. Wishing your life would just be easier and having everyone pity you when really you should be grateful for every breath you take in. But my views of the world all changed that summer day in the park.

Reading my book I barely looked up as someone took the seat beside me on the bench. I glanced up to see a young boy of about fifteen smiling at me. The way his blonde hair shone in the sunlight caught my attention and I placed my book on my lap.

"Excuse me, my name is Grant, and I was wondering if you would like to share my lunch with me?"

Surprised by this kind and generous offer given to me from a complete stranger I did not answer for a moment. He took this lapse in silence to pull out a picnic basket.

"Sure," I finally responded, "Although I must say it is kind of weird that you just offer a stranger something to eat."

"Well we wouldn't be strangers if I knew your name."

"Right, of course," I stammered, "Sam Nelson."

"It is my pleasure to meet you Sam."

Before I knew it he grabbed my hand and kissed it. That is when disaster forced its way into my happy little life. A light flashed before my eyes and I jumped up. My head was in a whirlwind of images and all of a sudden they formed a clear picture. It was Grant walking home from the park. The pain of the vision was so intense that I was aware I had started to scream.

Grant suddenly stopped walking and headed down a dark ally. A man clothed in black came up to him and they exchanged something. Quickly Grant ran off in the other direction.

I closed my eyes thinking the image would go away but it didn't. It was inside of my head forcing its way into every crevice of my mind until I had nowhere to hide from it and had to face it. Grant was running from the man when all of a sudden he gave a shout.

"You filthy little liar, I told you it was going to be two hundred! This is just a twenty wrapped around some ones!"

Desperate Grant tried to flee from the man but he was not fast enough. The gun shot echoed throughout the alley and Grant dropped to the ground like a lead weight. The man ran off into the distance and disappeared. A searing white light passed in front of my eyes and I blacked out.

I woke up lying on my back behind the bench. I got up slowly not sure if the pain was going to return. I looked at my watch, it was almost midnight. Oh god, my mom is going to kill me but I had to see if Grant was alright or if I was just going crazy.

The clock outside the diner where Grant was going to meet Mr. had said twelve ten. I had seen that street before. It was two houses down from mine and I lived about three blocks away from the park. I gathered my things and ran for it, there was still time to stop this and save a life. At an empty street I spotted him walking hurriedly forward with his hood up covering his face.

"Grant," I yelled to him but he could not hear me. I was running out of steam, my breathing labored, made a loud noise in the eerily deserted street. I ran forward and stopped dead. The shot ran out against the quite night and Grant fell into view, blood pooling out of him.

"No!" I screamed but it was all too late. A woman screamed and five minutes later I saw police cars drive up surrounding me, cradling Grant's head in my lap.

My mother picked me up at the police station after they were done questioning me.

"Sam! Oh god Sam I thought you were hurt! What happened here?" In a daze I walked past her to the car where I sat and cried.

That was when I first realized I could see a glimpse into the future. This little monster inside of my head did not go away and the visions did not stop as I got older. I finally accepted it. The visions were completely random, sometimes I saw things that would happen a minute later, sometimes years.

Not everything had to do with a person's death. When I was sixteen I sat at a restaurant eating. When I grabbed my check my hand lightly slid against the waiter's. A moment passed and when I went to leave I called to her, "Don't forget to turn the oven off." The girl gave me a look and claimed she wouldn't. That day I had been in time to stop an impending disaster, others I had not been.

In May I was eighteen and I was getting used to the gift. That is when my world flipped upside down. I had learned that the visions only occurred when I came into contact with another person. Although I had figured that out some people were immune to my touch. My mother was one of the people, that for years I could come in contact with and not get any visions. I thought that she was just another person that happened to be defective, or so I thought.

Sitting on the couch I reached across her to get my drink I had left on the table. My arm lightly brushed her hand lying so gently on the couch when it hit me. Usually I am able to control myself in public and my visions had gotten a lot less painful. But this one hit me like the force of a semi-truck. I froze and the glass dropped out of my hand shattering on the floor.

"Sam!" My mother yelled jumping up and running to the kitchen. I fell to the floor my hands on my head moaning. "Sam. Sam can you hear me what's wrong!"

I could vaguely hear my mother's voice outside of my head with all the pain. I screamed when the vision came into focus sending pain throughout my body. My mother was in the hospital. Except it wasn't her, it looked as if something else had crawled into her body and had drained her of life. He eyes were sunken in and she was pale. Sweat glistened on her forehead and her breathing was labored. A doctor came into the room a look of fear and sadness across his face.

"Ms. Nelson I am sorry to say this but you have an inoperable brain tumor. You only have three weeks to live. We can give you medicine to reduce the pain but we can't hold it off any longer, I am so sorry."

My mother took all of this in with a calm expression. The vision faded out and I awoke on the floor tears streaming down my face.

I confided everything in my mother. I told her about my gift and what I had seen. She took it all in still very worried about me.

"No, no you don't understand you are going to die! And there is nothing anyone can do to stop it," I wailed.

"It's ok honey," she replied, a calm expression plastered on her face.

The next day she went to the doctor and my worst fears were confirmed. They gave her one year to live. She came home to me with a smile on her face.

"Honey, thank you. Thank you and thank god for giving me notice. I have so much to do and so little time."

"No mom," I pleaded with her, "We can fix this. Fate can be changed."

"No, if it is my time to go then I have no objection to that at all."

I have to do something. I can't let her die. That night around midnight I grabbed my jacket and climbed out the window.

The knock on the door echoed through the house.

"Come on. Come on," I whispered, "Please be there."

The door creaked open an inch and revealed a sleepy sea green eye. Scarlet and I had met after I had my first vision. She had confronted me in the police station and had told me about the gift. You see there are more people out there like me. We walk among ordinary people; they are oblivious of us and our knowledge.

"What are you doing here I told you never to meet me at my house unless it was an emergency."

"It's my mother. She has cancer and she is going to die. I need to fix her and change her destiny."

Scarlet sighed and led me to the kitchen. "You are in no hurry, now sit down and have something to eat."

"You see Sam, there are rules to the gift. No using the visions as a personal gain, you can't tell people of our secret organization, and you cannot interfere with the visions. You may warn the person of the upcoming incident but you can't intervene yourself."

"When will I be old enough to be in the group?"

"Soon," Scarlet said putting her bronze hand on top of mine. The odd thing about Scarlet is that even with her dark skin and dark hair she has the most beautiful blue eyes in the world.

She blinked her heavy eyelashes at me, "Don't sweat it honey, you will learn in your lifetime to let go of the people in your life and become one of our little family."

"No!" I shouted jumping up from my chair. "I will not give up hope on her, not now not ever!"

I ran to the park where it had all began. Crying I lay on a bench and fell asleep. Even though I knew I could never save my mother, I had to try. But no matter what I did I never could outrun destiny. I had gained my mother a few more years of her life but it was effortless. Eventually my mother's health started to deteriorate and she was put into the hospital. I, being 21, was old enough to be living on my home. My mother left all of our possessions to me and I was able to afford to go to college.

That night was just how my vision said it would be. At the funeral Scarlet came up and embraced me.

"Come now, it is time to join the group. We will teach you all we know and you will roam the earth with us. Who knows one day we may be able to show those idiots in the government something that will send them running from us."

I stepped away from her. "Are you talking about getting into the government and using your gift as a personal gain?"

"Don't look at it like that; see it as an improvement of our great country. You know there are more people with gifts out there. They are not like us but they can contribute to the cause and one day we can put those filthy humans in their place. No longer will we be teased or ridiculed."

"How can you say such things, you were a human once. You had a human life and human family. What ever happened to that?"

"I shed away my human life and my human family. They were just dragging me down. You are already halfway there. Now come join us and you will be accepted."

Rage bubbled forth from me like a volcano. I swung at her face and made contact with her jaw. In that instant everything changed. I knew I had to stop her and I had to do it soon. The fate of the free human race depended on whether Scarlet's plan was carried out. Fate can be changed and it was my duty to do it. Scarlet got up vengeance in her eyes.

"You will regret the decision. We live forever you know, because of our gift. It is a long time to be without people who truly understand you."

"You could never understand me!" I spat at her in disgust.

"You will be sorry. I will make you sorry." She stalked to her car and sped off into the night. I knew what I had to do and I would not give up until she did.

Sometimes I wonder how my death will happen. I assumed Scarlet was right when she said I would live for a very long time. In these past years I have been chasing Scarlet across the world. I would not let the vision I had of her become a reality. In the years of my search I discovered a power of telepathy. I practiced in the months on the road and became a skilled master at moving objects. When the time came I would be prepared for Scarlet.

I found her in a motel on a late December morning. Two guards were posted outside her door. I used the vending machine next to them to incapacitate them. They cried as they fell down crushed under the heavy machine. Scarlet gasped when I entered the room.

"What are you going to do now Sam? Are you going to kill me? Frankly you don't have the guts. Hanging around with humans all your life you couldn't be expected to know how to react appropriately. You weren't the person I thought you were."

"Scarlet I am glad I never lived up to your expectations," I replied, pacing in front of her. "I would never want to give up my soul for a gift like yours."

I grabbed her face in my hands and concentrated until an image formed in my mind. A bright hot white flashed inside my head. It would happen tomorrow at dusk. She would be driving along a winding road when an aggressive driver would cut her off. Swerving she would try to get her car under control but fail. Plunging off the ledge of the mountain side she would meet her untimely doom as so many others had done in her hands. I sent the image into Scarlet's mind. I don't really know how I did it but I knew what I did had dire consequences to it.

Scarlet screamed as she received the image and it became part of her reality. At long last I released her head and fell to the floor gasping for breath.

"No, no!! It won't happen, I won't let it happen!"

I slowly got to my feet feeling woozy and drained. "Scarlet, don't you know you can't change fate. It will happen and you will die. It is just how your destiny is written."

I heard her blood curdling scream as I walked out the door to my car. I knew what I had designed for her would come true. There is no way you can escape your fate.

As for me what I did had dire consequences. One thing Scarlet was right about were the rules. I had changed the destiny of another person so I lost my powers. Sometimes I find myself longing for them in the dark hours of the night. I feel lost and complete at the same time. I can now lead a normal life with mine and others' destiny unaware to everyone. I will never forget Scarlet and all that she has taught me. Even being the traditional evil villain in my life's story she taught me valued lesson. Life is supposed to have mystery in it. Fate is a mistress that should not be tempted, who knows what surprises she holds for us in our future.

Allie and her brothers

From left: Bryan, Allie, Chris and Joe Jr. on the Oregon Coast 2011

Poetry

Untitled #11

long ears, fuzzy toes
bunny tail & bunny nose

Alice leaned closer for a look
One breath was all it took

Falling falling out of control
down a wild rabbit hole

Lost in a strange land
which was ruled by a strict hand

Angry caterpillar's advice
and Tea with the Hatter was far from nice

Cookies & mushrooms are just not food
While the Cheshire cat was quite rude

Odd creatures in the forest
The red queen was the ultimate test

You'll never know what you'll find
when in a child's dreaming mind

**Allie @ Bellingham Bay
in Bellingham, WA 2008**

Step One

Step One
To the edge of the building
Step two –
Two steps
To get closer
Feel the wind
Across your face
Step three
Three breaths
Deeply inhaling
The air of life
Sounds below
Rush by
Step four
Four moments
Of regret
Of sorrow
Of guilt
Of no tomorrow
Step five
Five seconds
Of falling free
Feeling free
Happy
Step six
Six people
Mourn the boy
That took
One step

Untitled #12

Lights blinking, twinkling
I feel myself shrinking
besides a giant so big
& wonderful.

The night sky swallows me
so dark & vast I can barely see
pinpoints of light
that glow & shine & fight
to be seen.
to be noticed.

Small lights in the sky
make me feel tiny as I try
to imagine their world
a strange new place.

I watch them every night
Can they ever show me light?
a truly happy place
somewhere out in space?
take me away from reality

I reach out, pleading
I cry out, needing
something better
somewhere good

I drop my hands slowly
the stars were never meant for me
just bright objects in the sky
watching my life go by

But sometimes I wonder
late at night
that someday I might
touch those lights

Untitled #13

you look
at me & I
look back. you
& I. Him & you.
He turns your face &
you smile. I want to know
that smile. I've seen it but
I want to know it. Him & you.
You & I. You look at me as you walk
by. Whisper with your eyes, "I see you."
I think you see me. But I'll never see you.
I look away & breathe. Him and her. You and me.
That's the way it should be. I'll mend you again.
I'll hold your hand. It won't ever be. It will only be
Him & you. And me. Just me. Will my love ever be
enough? You & he look past me. Look through me & see
nothing is there. Even if you stare you can't see,
the reason that I am me. You keep my eyes
as he says goodbye. Don't see me cry. Within myself
is where I hide. Just you & I.

I see
your face
every day.
Look into those
eyes. Him & me.
You & I. Why can't
it be you & I? Why?
I look at your face
& see something inside.
I see it, but I'll never
know it. Look away but
you'll still stay inside my
mind. Him & Her. You & I. You
can hold me as I cry. But still

I stand quietly by. I'll just be
here looking into your eyes. Can you
see? Can you really see me? Will you
ever know what we can be? If only
we could try. I look away. Him. Me. You.
He says goodbye & I lie. What I really want is you.
You & I

Untitled #14

Crash
& boom
like thunder
inside my head.
Get out. Please
leave now. I can't
take your judgment.
can't take the torment.
knives to my wrists won't
make it stop. A bullet can
make me drop. Stone cold & you'll
be dead. Yes just one bullet to my head. No more whining. Crying.
Begging to be let out. You chose this route.
it's all your fault. You're the one that called.
took me by the brain. drove me insane.
At least that's what they say. Insane
tomorrow & today. I wish you'd leave.
Please, just please. go away. and away
you stay. Indecision, incomplete. Folks
get a front row seat. Kid is gonna
blow his head. the voices will
soon be fed. Hungry cries
in my ears. Screaming
my insecurities & fears.
the gun is lifted
placed & cocked
and now I
see, the
thing I
hate is
me

Untitled #15

look up & see
what is there for me
up in the sky
way up high
can't wait til I go
either fast or slow
up to the sky I look
please take this soul I took
no heaven is left
not after this theft
I stole a life
with the blade of a cold knife
I will never rest
please lord can I confess
my immortal sin
let this begin
judgment today
judge me every way
choose to keep
what is meant for the street
or let me go
down to hell below
heaven or hell
I can't really tell
either is fine
because I'm one of a kind.

Untitled #16

i think i am falling in
love. How did it happen? One day
i was fine, now i feel as if i need
this other person to survive. Weak
at the knees, dry throat, what in the
hell is wrong with me? I am smiling
all the time & it's a wonderfully scary
feeling. Whomever thought of
love must have been either genius
or fool. i am undecided as to which.
Can't sleep, dreaming the sweetest
dreams. A friend at school, does
he see what is hidden under
my politeness & lame jokes? Sitting
across at lunch i beg his eyes to
wander over to me, catch my eyes
& hold them. At a glance not the
best, but once you get past, wonderful.
Now i realize what everyone loves
about high school. Can this feeling
last? I very much
hope so.

love,
Allison

Minooka High[17]

Heartache is nearby.

Is he telling me lies?

Gone is the innocence we know,

Having been replaced by inappropriate clues.

Scanning the cafeteria for your table.

Convincing yourself you're more than capable in

Handling these honors classes.

Overworking your tired asses.

Orange and black, yeah we rule.

Living one more year through high school.

---

[17] Allie attended Minooka High School from 2008 – 2011. Two scholarship funds in her name offer aspiring authors and animal scientists a financial boost for college. For more information, contact Minooka High School at www.mchs.net

Untitled #17

A child sits on the kitchen floor
hiding under the table.
His father takes a step away
From his mother lying
Crying on the floor.

A little boy looks down
at his feet while the others
eat the food they brought.
His stomach aches & hurts
as he looks at the scraps
he managed to get off the ground.

A student stands in front
of a high school class room.
He fidgets & pulls
at his sweatshirt sleeves
Trying to hide
the bruises on his arms

A young man walks across
the streets of the city.
An old woman is standing
shivering against the cold as
the men take her purse away.
A young man continues to walk.

A man stands quietly
At a cemetery
A flag is folded and lain
on the casket on a soldier.
Snow falls on the funeral,
on the young bride, the family,
the best friend.

A man takes a drink &
stumbles through the door.
A man yells in the darkness
A man grabs a woman
and throws her to the ground.
A man takes his anger, hurt,
 betrayal
& uses them, weapons of life
beat at the woman
lying, crying on the floor
A child peeks
around the bedroom door
A man stops and drops
to his knees
The silence rises up and
the world hears the cries
of a broken man.

The Dance

Hot and cramped behind the curtain
The makeup is painted on me like a clown.
Waiting, waiting, waiting for my turn
to burst on stage, and hope I don't fall down.

inside my stomach tumbles
The lights are hot on the stage
The music starts to rumble
I feel like I am trapped in a cage

Wanting to burst forward, wanting to fly
My nerves are twisted like a bow
Wanting to dance and be free until I die
I can't believe it is my turn to go.

Running on, I dare not look up
into the sea of eyes staring at me.
I have to keep calm, I cannot get stuck
a smile, deep breaths, that is the key

Suddenly the nerves melt away
I am brilliant, I am good
No longer worried about what to do or what to say
I let the dance pour from me like a flood.

Music fades off, breathing is hard
Audience applauds and cameras flash
happy and excited, I release my guard
and all my fears fly away with a dash

Fear

My heart is racing.
My throat tightens.
The cold feeling is constantly chasing,
anything that can brighten
my mind and soul.
A helpless, hopeless abyss.
I am slowly falling into the hole
Will I never again experience his sweet kiss?
The darkness is surrounding,
the walls rise up, towering above.
My fists are pounding
against a wall of bitter love.
Nowhere to turn, nowhere to go.
I am completely surrounded but utterly alone
It is all over, I know,
but I still can hope for the unknown.
The mysteries of life that lie before me
are the source from which my fear springs.
And I know however hard I plea,
I will have to face whatever the future brings.
Shivers run down my spine.
When will this be over?
I have reached & strived for the divine,
being a believer.
But have struggled and failed
at everything I had dreamed.
My casket is now nailed
and no matter how I screamed,
the fear is inside now.
The darkness is closing in.
Sweat pours down my brow.
It is time to face my sin.

My Tears

Tears are contagious.
Why is it true
that when I cry...
you do too?
Tears are contagious
I find it hard
to keep my face dry
When lowering my guard.
it's not my fault,
really I try.
to keep my emotions in
when I see you cry.
but something just happens
deep inside
that when it occurs,
the tears I can't hide.
tears are contagious,
people tell me so.
but maybe it's just me,
that makes the tears flow.

Untitled #18

This is a poem
What is it about?
it's about you
it's about me
it's about creativity.
I've got some ideas
spinning round my head
I must write them down
or I will forget, I dread.
it can be looong
or short,
small
& sweet.
it can be messy.
or it can be neat.
No matter where I am
with a paper & pen
I can make a poem
with a beginning & an end.

Where am I now?
At a grocery store.
I think I'll write a poem
about some eggs, maybe 4
under a tree
friends sitting beside me.
what a wonderful place
for a writer to be.

At the dentist
mouth full of cotton
wish I can write a poem
about an eagle, on a mountain

Allison

A stubborn girl with books and friends
giving laughter to all of them
loves alone time with a good book
or enjoying t.v. shows with a stare or a look
no sisters, but a cousin like a flower
always there is Rachael Fleshauer
fears the crawly thing at night
gets dizzy when looking from heights
wants to travel to Greece or Rome
but when needed always goes back home
listens to other peoples' troubles
but afterwards feels overwhelmed, all times double

**Allie in Puerto Vallarta, Mexico
2009**

Allie

Lazy girl at the age of 15
       shy and funny to her friends
strong beliefs in the rights
       of animals & women

trusting in the one she loves
       to always be with her
hoping to see them all
       even when she's older

truthful yet kind
       and fair to all people
far away at times
       but attentive when needed

Allie in Vancouver, Canada 2011

In The Corner

There is a creature in the corner
Of my room. And there he sits.
There is a thing in the corner
Of my room. and there he ticks.

Tick Tick
Scratch

There is a fright in the corner
Of my room. To you I cry!
There is a growl in the corner
Of the room. I do not lie!

Growl Growl
Snap

There is a menace in the corner
Of my room. Please, come and
   see!
There is a terror in the corner
Of my room. Come, before he gets
   me!

Do you hear him creak?
Creak
Creak
Squeak

Long Nails!
Thirteen Tails!
Seven Eyes!
These aren't lies!

There is a monster in the corner
Of my room. And there he bites.

Snap Snap

There is nothing in the corner
Of my room in the morning light.
…
But wait
Until tonight.

Tired

Sleeping
Sleep
Sleep

Dozing off and dreaming as
Images float past.

Breathing
In
Out

All is calm and peaceful when
This is the bed that I am in.

Softly
Tucked
In

The world at night is slowing down
My thoughts stop spinning round.

Stretching
Yawn
Sigh

I have never appreciated sleep,
Until here I lay and count the sheep.

The Addict

The Rush,
It's Burning through my Veins.

The High,
It's Clouding in my Brain.

Elation,
Feels like I'm going Insane

Eventually it wears off,
I'm left exhausted.
I can't help thinking about,
The next time I can do it again.

The Rush,
This is the most Fun.

The High,
My all-time favorite Season.

Elation,
I can see no Rhyme or Reason.

And through it all,
I can't help thinking,
Is this what they call
An Addiction?

Life Sayings

"Oh, I thought you said bandana." – Rebecca Deluga

"AT&T gives me heartburn." – Oz

"It's too early in the morning for these shenanigans." – Anonymous

"Diet Dr. Pepper tastes like cupcakes." – Drew

"I have no force. I'm not a Jedi." – Me

"Whisper whisper whisper" – Me & Nicole

"Ow I think I just broke my toe." – Hailey Evens

"You should have worn your safety goggles." – Me

"I try & try but he never wants to hear me out" – bathroom stall

"You hit the jackpot mo-fo!" – Ruth quoting comedian

"Start guessing obvious things." – Bryan

"Are you Trisha?" "Jim." – bathroom stall

"Nathan you have to wear your clothes." – Me

"I just forgot how to speak Spanish." – Cynthia

"Salad area" – Trash can

"How do you impress people without sacrificing your beliefs?" – bathroom stall

"But a sentence can mean enough, it can do enough" – "The Last Rung on the Ladder," by Stephen King

"You don't need a death sentence to live your life." – Mr. Brown

Day to Day

Muscles aching
legs shaking
headache rising
time is flying
      by me

Yawn escapes me
hunger takes me
tangible proof
to never tell the truth
about my lying
about my trying
      to make ends meet.

All day earning
all day turning
my time is burning
my heart is churning
      to get to you.

Can't help wishing,
but time keeps inching
along the day
can't wait to say
      I love you

Finally done
want to shout, want to run
all the way home
the quicker I get from
      here to you

Door is open
wishes well spoken
give you my love, my heart
can't bear being apart
      from you

Sun in the sky
I just want to lie
right here with you
but I have to get through
      another day

Kiss you sweetly
love you completely
another day start
another day end
don't want to part
but I'll do it all again
      for you

Untitled #19

"Did you see that?" he gasped. "She sneezed."
A father holds his girl close. Right
now is his happiest moment. No
other woman would be able to
have such a hold on him, to be
able to change the way he
thinks about life. The squirming
baby in his arms is his daughter
and he will never let her go.

"Hold on tight honey!"
He yells after her worried,
he chases after her pink bike
ready to catch her if she falls.
He will always be there, running
close behind, hands outstretched
& strong. She can always count
on him. He'll never
let her go.

"Hands on the
wheel & buckle up. Call me after
you get there."
She drives off. Young & eager.
He has taught her a lesson she
will never forget. He looks
after the car, watching until she
is gone. He rushes inside & waits
by the phone. When she calls, he
will be relieved, but until then he
waits. Whatever might happen, he
will be there. He'll never let her
go.

"You're beautiful." He whispers
in her ear. The wedding gown fits

perfectly & she is an angel. Now
everyone can see her as he sees
her. Perfect. He walks slowly, holding
her tightly. Time is almost up &
he doesn't want to let go. Even
though she's getting married,
she is still his baby girl.
And he will never let her go.

She walks in. He stirs slightly
in his sleep. His breathing is
ragged & shallow. She sinks into the
seat next to him. Fond memories
flood her. She takes his frail hand
& realizes that this might be
the last time. The last time she
can hold her father's hand.
How wonderful that a man like
this can change her life. That he
can be the only man that
matters to a young girl & help
shape her view of the world.
He stirs & looks over to her. He
smiles. She wipes her eyes & gives
him a kiss. She leans &
whispers, "I love you daddy, I'll
never let go."

Untitled #20

I hold you in my hands & smile
how I love a book
full of fantasies & alternate realities.
something to hold in your hand.
a portable adventure.
I crack open your title page
just to peek in.
uniform & right,
your words bring so much comfort
to my world.
boring turns to excitement
reality gives way to something…
better
something fantastic.
I settle down into your words,
your stories.
Now I don't need technology
no Kindle or Nook
can ever replace the quality
of a tangible book.

Untitled #21

the plot thickens
main characters arise
something dramatic happens
there before my eyes.
A little romance
& some violent fights
giving them a chance
before the brightening of the lights.
show me something good
something I never knew would
touch my heart or cause
make me smile or should
leave me wild & wanting
something more
scary part is coming
& I'll hide my face
the villain is running
people gone without a chase
there is something exciting
about going to the movies.

Untitled #22

Get up!
let's play!
spin around
before falling down
come on!
let's play!
dance in the rain
& never regret it
while living with the pain.
Hold my hand
& we'll play!
make believe
& princesses
put on our fancy dresses.
You'll be king & I the queen
nothing is as it seems
Please!
let's play!
come run with me
just because we can
grow young with me.
here take my hand
never grow up
you'll just get stuck
in a dead end job
you'll become a snob
& you won't play
please just today
Act young and free
and stay with me

Untitled #23

take a deep breath
lean in close
never let me go

I'm not sure what love is
and I can't really tell you
why I feel this way.
but let's close our eyes
& forever stay
in love

I never noticed my happiness before
it was just there
& sometimes I feel that I might
die from your love
a happy death it will be
& then they'll see
our love.

snuggle up to me
kiss me sweetly
never let me go

dark nights
light up when I see you
brighter than the sunniest day
in summertime
when you said you loved me
I cried because the feeling I had
I knew it would last

right now
I can still see
your love
now we got older
& time always flies

but I never thought I would have to
say good bye

I wanted you to see
you have given me everything
& I want to say
thank you
and…please stay

it's late now
you'll be gone soon
so before you go
I'll take a deep breath
lean in closer
hold you tight
love you the most

Me

You made me believe in anger,
Always at your hands.
You made me believe in sadness,
Nothing here can ever change.
You made me learn violence
Hate
Revenge
It never seems to end,
A circle of depression with no
    particular
Mission of hate, lust, and envy.
You never believed me,
Listened or heard
Never said a word.

You made me believe in evil.
You made me believe in you.

He changed it all,
Caught me when I was about to
    fall,
Off this building
You had been making.

He made me believe in trust
That I must
Never hide away again.
He was my best friend,
Lover and soul mate.
Him you could never take.

He made me believe in happy,
Not always sappy or crappy,
But real,
Something I could feel,
With my mending heart,
That you ripped apart.

He made me believe in love,
Taught me not to shove,
Away the best thing ever.
He showed me what I never,
Saw until I left you.

He made me see me,
And he made me believe.

Untitled #24

Life seems so orderly sometimes
you go
along with no distractions
no problems.
You breathe in…and out. Just the
way you're supposed to
everything
seems to be going well. You're
    content.
not happy. But just as
close as you'll
ever be. And that's good for you.
At least it won't end
badly
But then
something
disrupts
your order
Things
in your
life just
CRACK now you're feeling all
    topsie turned.[18]
you try to right the words
but they just won't obey.
you're happy, sad, mad, excited,
    lonely and blissful
Things are crazy.
But in such a good way that
you need to tell yourself to stop
smiling.
you might be scaring people.

you miss your order
and you get close to coming back
but just like every other time
when you feel secure and safe
things tilt & swerve & you
CRACK

---

[18] Editor's note: In her handwritten
journal, Allison experimented with this
poem, jogging words about the page
starting at this line.

Untitled #25

Look at this fancy funeral here
Look at you all dressed in black
Look at Aunt Sally, the poor
dear
You're here for me, that's a fact
You all have come here to cry
and talk about how I died
But still, I wonder why
Why you put on those clothes
Nice pants and pressed shirts
Why do you put on these shows
When every word that you say
    hurts
Why did you clean up your face
And put makeup on those eyes
Why do you show not one trace
Of the person who frequently
    cries
I guess I get it
I understand
It's a tradition, it seems
To be formal at a funeral

It's what society deems
Normal
However, can't you see
That I don't care what you wear
As long as you're here for me
So, my darling
Yes, you my dear
Can I finally say what I want
    you to hear?
Please take off those shoes
I know they hurt your feet
And please, wear whatever you
    choose
And baby,
Darling,
My dear
Mourn me
Miss me
And always know I'm near
There is no need to put on an act
Just love me like you would
And after time – don't look back

Untitled #26

Don't compare me
to your perfect girl
don't compare me
to the beautiful
the artful
& smart
don't judge me
based on what you see
My ethnicity
My body
don't evaluate
my every score,
grade & test
don't put me
next to the best
and most of all
don't think you know me
don't think you
recognize
the girl
in disguise

Untitled #27

I miss you
your face and eyes
I wish you'd
come on by
I'd kiss you
It's no lie
that I love you
a love that won't die

Remember

Can't sleep tonight,
Couldn't sleep yesterday either.

I still can remember
When u were in my arms.
I couldn't save you,
Couldn't help.
I remember how hard it was
Not seeing your face,
Not knowing your fate.
I remember my guilt,
Always hanging above me.
Seeping into my life in flashes.
Flashes of memory,
So bright they blind.
I remember the day,
That dreadful day,
Where I saw you
So still, smooth face,
No voice, no life.
I remember how I cried,

How I had to cry,
To extinguish the burning of my
    soul.
I remember the ceremony,
Me in black, you in blue.
The tears of your life falling,
But none from me,
You took my tears when you left.
I remember when you told me you
    hated me,
I remember when you told me you
    loved me,
I remember when you told me you
    were leaving,
I remember when you asked me
    not to go.
I remember.

Can't sleep tonight.
Couldn't sleep yesterday either.

In Loving Memory Of
Allison M. Rivera
September 19, 1993
October 22, 2011

REMEMBER
BY: ALLISON RIVERA

Can't sleep tonight,
Couldn't sleep yesterday either.

I still can remember
When you were in my arms.
I couldn't save you,
Couldn't help.
I remember how hard it was
Not seeing your face,
Not knowing your fate.
I remember my guilt,
Always hanging above me.
Seeping into my life in flashes.
Flashes of memory,
So bright they blind.
I remember the day,
That dreadful day,
Where I saw you
So still, smooth face,
No voice, no life.
I remember how I cried,
How I had to cry,
To extinguish the burning of my soul.
I remember the ceremony,
Me in black, you in blue.
The tears of your life falling,
But none from me,
You took my tears when you left.
I remember when you told me you hated me,
I remember when you told me you love me,
I remember when you told me you were leaving,
I remember when you asked me not to go.
I remember.

Can't sleep tonight.
Couldn't sleep yesterday either.

Allie's Memorial Service Card

8.28.11 #1

Is this escapable
this fate I'm feeling?
Tired & ill
is this all fleeting?
My eyes are dull
My heart is aching
My brain searches
What is this meaning?
This everlasting pain
Pain beyond my seeing.
All I think
through every day
every thought I have
every breath I take
every moment passed
is how much longer
will all this last?

8.28.11 #2

I take one step toward you.
You throw me to the ground.
grind me to pieces,
pieces scattered all around.
Around me are tears
Tears of mine & yours.
You cry & apologize
Apologizing for another night
Nights spent drinking.
Drinking in your words,
words fill my head
Head pounding & mouth bleeding,
bleeding all the love away.
Away from you I run.
Running to anyone new.
New hope that can never be ruined.
A ruined family lies on the ground
Grinding into the night.
Tonight will change
changing every part of me.

Act Your Age!

Why can't you just
Act your age
Why can't you just
Be mature
Why can't you
Be nice
Be civil
Why can't you just
Let it go
Why can't you just
Leave it alone
Why can't you
Go on
Move ahead
Why can't you just
Act your age
Why can't you just
Be an adult
Why can't you
Grow up
Stop fighting
Be a parent
Listen
STOP

Why can't you just
Stop

Everything that I am

I am a tiger
Strong and able
Hunting day and night
Dangerous to all

I am a hummingbird
Twittering through the day
Wings going a mile a minute
So fast, I'm invisible

I am a bear
Not the fastest, but strong
Protective and loving
But playful in my own nature

I am an owl
Wisdom is my partner
Awake at night
Wide eyes searching the forest
    floor

I am
I am

I am human
Vulnerable but intelligent
I am a daughter
I am a friend
I am love
I am hate
I am hope
I am death
I am me
I am you

I am
I am

Allie, age 17, at home

Allie, age 17, Christmas 2010

If I had a little money

Money isn't everything
I know it's true
But it may make some of my
   dreams come true

With a little money
I could get a car
A shiny, fast, zooming, speedy car

With a little money
I could get a house
A big, spacious, luxurious,
   mansion-like house

With a little money
I could get a pet
A loyal, loving, sweet, soft pet

With a little money
Just a little bit of money

I could make them stop fighting
Yelling, screaming, hitting,
   leaving

With a little money
I could make her smile
Happy, laughing, loving, sweet
   smiles

With a little money
I could make him come back
Staying, holding, hugging, missing
   me

With a little money
I could make a family
Constant, caring, loving, blissful,
   sharing
Happy family

With a little money
Just a little bit of money.

Perfect World

A perfect scene unfurls,
In a perfect world.
Dinner on a table,
Everything fits the label,
Of a wonderful day,
Going on in a wonderful way.
Everything is good,
As it always should.
No one ever lies,
And no one ever dies.
Happy faces glow,
Only happiness to show.
In my perfect world,
I am safely curled.

But...wait.
I am not in the right state.
This is not a perfect world,
That I have unfurled.
It is not full of happiness
But it is emotionless.
Everyone lies,
And most certainly everyone dies.
No longer safe I shrink away.
The real world might be good today,
But I prefer to stay,
In my own perfect world.

The Faces in Me

How many faces do you have?
I have five. . . I think.
One for the morning,
She is staring at me from the mirror above the bathroom sink.
One for school,
She is attentive and good.
One for family,
She is sharing, I supposed she would.
One for friends,
She is playful and fun.
One for the haters,
She is strong, will not be outdone.
Two more I have remembered,
The most important two.
There is also one for me,
And there is one for you.

Untitled #28

Momma how'd you get so old?
Baby, I was born old.
Momma how'd you get so gray?
Baby, that's not gray hair, it's the ash
From the holocaust.
Momma how'd you get so tall?
Baby, I'm tall because I had to hold up
all them trees
Momma, how'd you get so strong?
Baby, I'm strong because I had to catch
the buildings when they fell.
Momma, how do you swim so good?
Baby, I can swim because I had to go
get the ships that were sinkin'.
Momma, how'd you get so smart?
Baby, I'm smart because I had to build bombs.
Momma, how'd you get so mean?
Baby, I'm mean because I have to kill
people to save others.

Now Baby, it's time for bed.
sigh.
Baby, how'd I get so old?

Against Me

Everyone's against me
I hate it so much
I can't please
I can't do right
Everyone's angry
Want some kind of power
And just me
In the middle
Of it all
Everyone's sad
Say they are trying
And why can't I
Do it too?
Everyone wants me
To do everything
For them
Against them
Never for me
Everyone's against me
I'm torn apart
No way I can be
Both judge
And jury
No one is with me
No one by my side
And that's because
Everyone's against me

Time Passes

I am a young girl, strong and healthy,
Good personality and fairly wealthy,
Only child with loving parents,
Dreaming of a country house with a white picket fence.
Time Passes
Rebellious teenager in pursuit of freedom,
I seek danger begging it to come.
My parents are angry, ashamed, and sad
The baby in my belly is growing. This will end bad.
Time Passes

My baby is crying, she needs to be fed.
I am living in the city, alone and unwed,
Looking for a job, trying to get by.
I have to come up with rent by the end of July.
Time Passes

I am lost in his eyes, a sea of deep blue,
Finally it is time to say 'I do.'
Walking down the aisle he is waiting for me
I follow after my little Marie.
My parents are crying tears of joy,
I know in my heart he is not just some boy.
Time Passes

Child grown up, going off to college,
Without her I don't know how I will manage.
A kiss on her cheek, a wave goodbye,
I slowly wipe away a tear from my eye.
Time Passes

Grandmother of three, I go to the doctor
Cancer of the blood is now my captor
How will I tell them? What can I do?
I cannot lie, I cannot tell the untrue

Time Passes

On my death bed, I am patiently waiting,
The pain is gone, it is no longer advancing.
I am ready to go; I have lived a full life,
Caring woman, mother, grandmother, and wife.
I have just one thought on how it all flew by,
Before I go, ascending to the sky.
They will mourn me, it will be hard,
But they will have to move on afterward.
In time they will forget, the pain will ease, their love amasses,
After all, in the end, Time Passes.

Allie in Sedona, AZ 2011

Fire and Ice

Some say the world will end in fire,
Some say in ice.
From what I've tasted of desire
I hold with those who favour fire.
But if it had to perish Twice,
I think I know enough of hate
To say that for destruction ice
Is also great
And would suffice.

The End

What will we do when it comes to the end?
Will we cry to the sky, yelling the prayers that we send?
What will we do when it is our time to part?
Will we quietly sit, or run away when forced to depart?
How will we face death staring at us?
We will drop to our knees, relying on our trust
Or will we bravely stand up and stand strong?
Will it hurt? Will it be long?
What will we do when the Earth dies away?
Will we regret our mistakes and wish to live another day?
What will we do when it is all over?
Will we reconcile our fights and to our family become closer?
What will you do when you are to be judged?
Will you cower away or on will you trudge,
Fighting your fears, the sins that you made?
Will you stand up strong and brilliant, or forever will you fade?

Allie in Las Vegas NV 2010

Allie at her National Honor
Society Awards

age 17

Love & Peace

love,
Allison